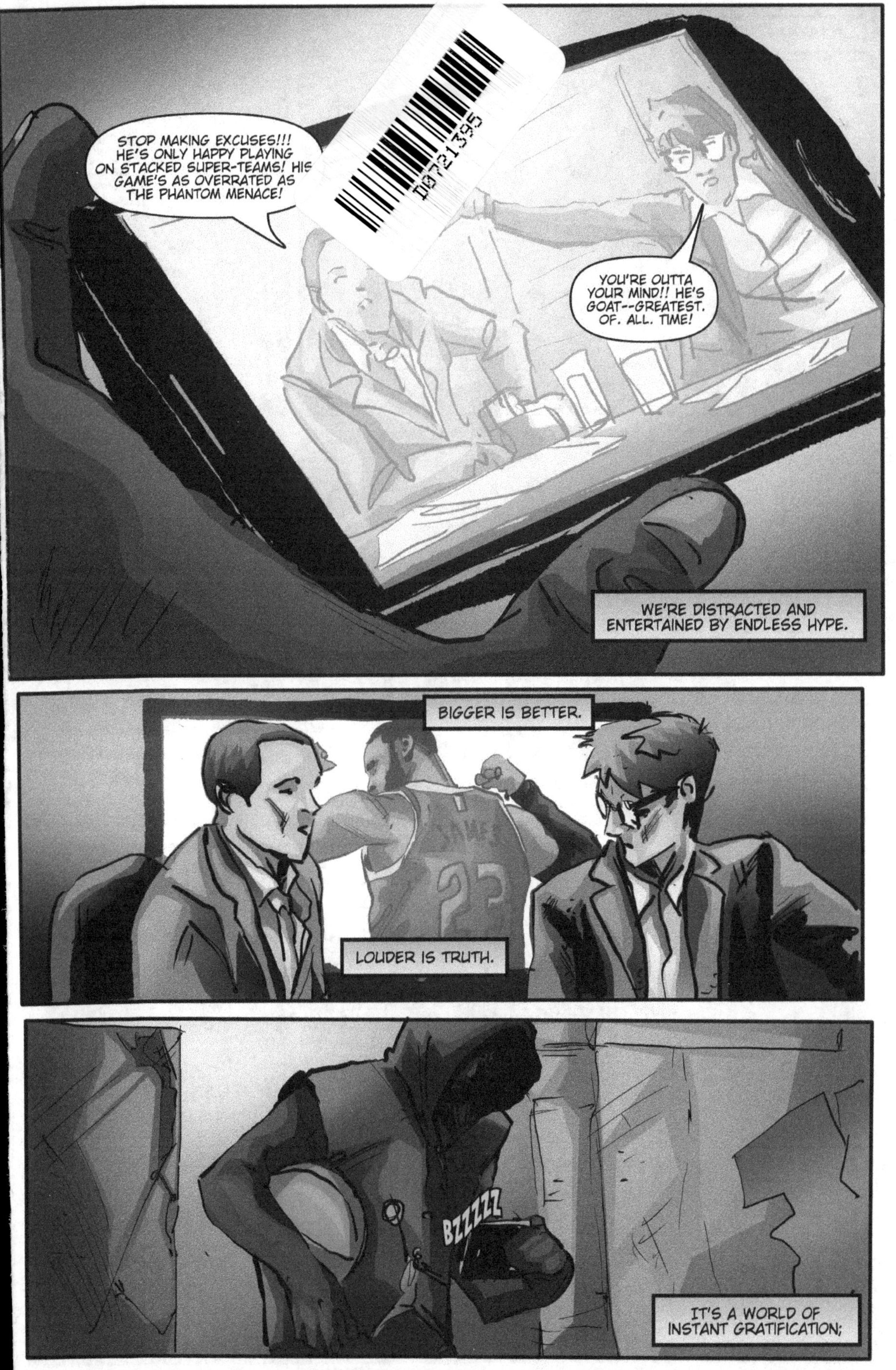

STOP MAKING EXCUSES!!! HE'S ONLY HAPPY PLAYING ON STACKED SUPER-TEAMS! HIS GAME'S AS OVERRATED AS THE PHANTOM MENACE!
YOU'RE OUTTA YOUR MIND!! HE'S GOAT--GREATEST. OF. ALL. TIME!
WE'RE DISTRACTED AND ENTERTAINED BY ENDLESS HYPE.
BIGGER IS BETTER.
LOUDER IS TRUTH.
BZZZZZ
IT'S A WORLD OF INSTANT GRATIFICATION;

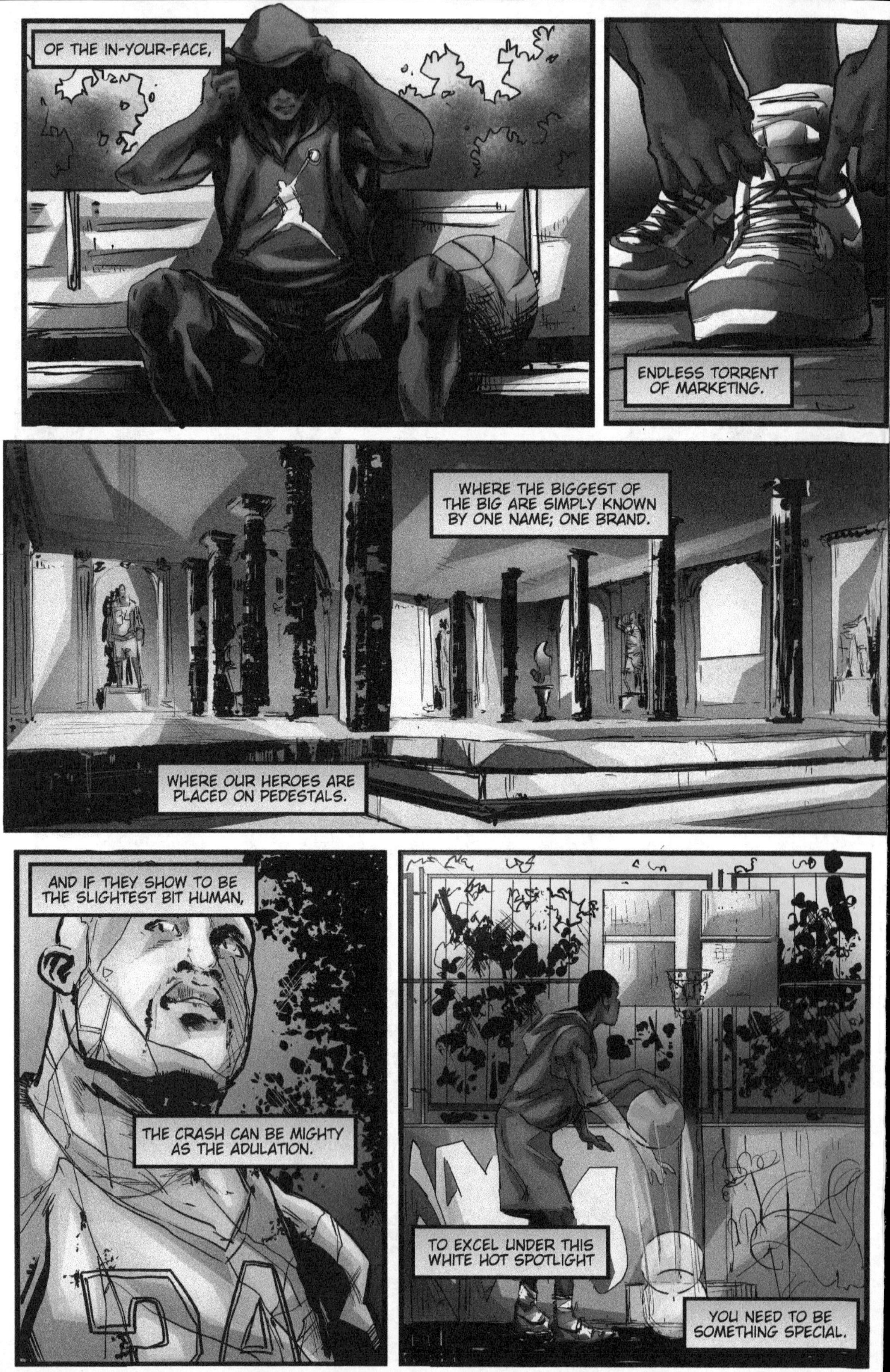
OF THE IN-YOUR-FACE,
ENDLESS TORRENT OF MARKETING.
WHERE THE BIGGEST OF THE BIG ARE SIMPLY KNOWN BY ONE NAME; ONE BRAND.
WHERE OUR HEROES ARE PLACED ON PEDESTALS.
AND IF THEY SHOW TO BE THE SLIGHTEST BIT HUMAN,
THE CRASH CAN BE MIGHTY AS THE ADULATION.
TO EXCEL UNDER THIS WHITE HOT SPOTLIGHT
YOU NEED TO BE SOMETHING SPECIAL.

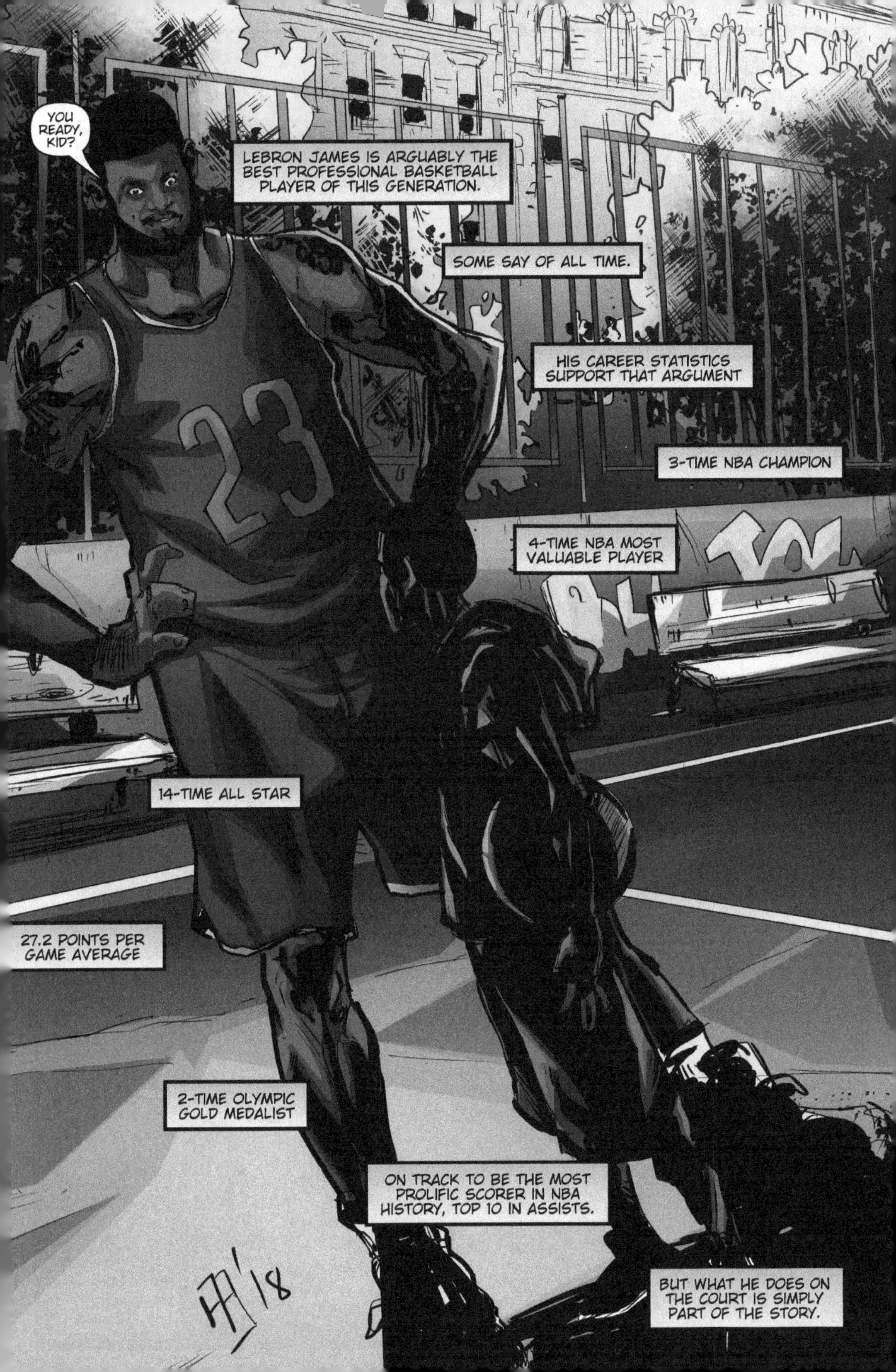

YOU READY, KID?
LEBRON JAMES IS ARGUABLY THE BEST PROFESSIONAL BASKETBALL PLAYER OF THIS GENERATION.
SOME SAY OF ALL TIME.
HIS CAREER STATISTICS SUPPORT THAT ARGUMENT
3-TIME NBA CHAMPION
4-TIME NBA MOST VALUABLE PLAYER
14-TIME ALL STAR
27.2 POINTS PER GAME AVERAGE
2-TIME OLYMPIC GOLD MEDALIST
ON TRACK TO BE THE MOST PROLIFIC SCORER IN NBA HISTORY, TOP 10 IN ASSISTS.
BUT WHAT HE DOES ON THE COURT IS SIMPLY PART OF THE STORY.

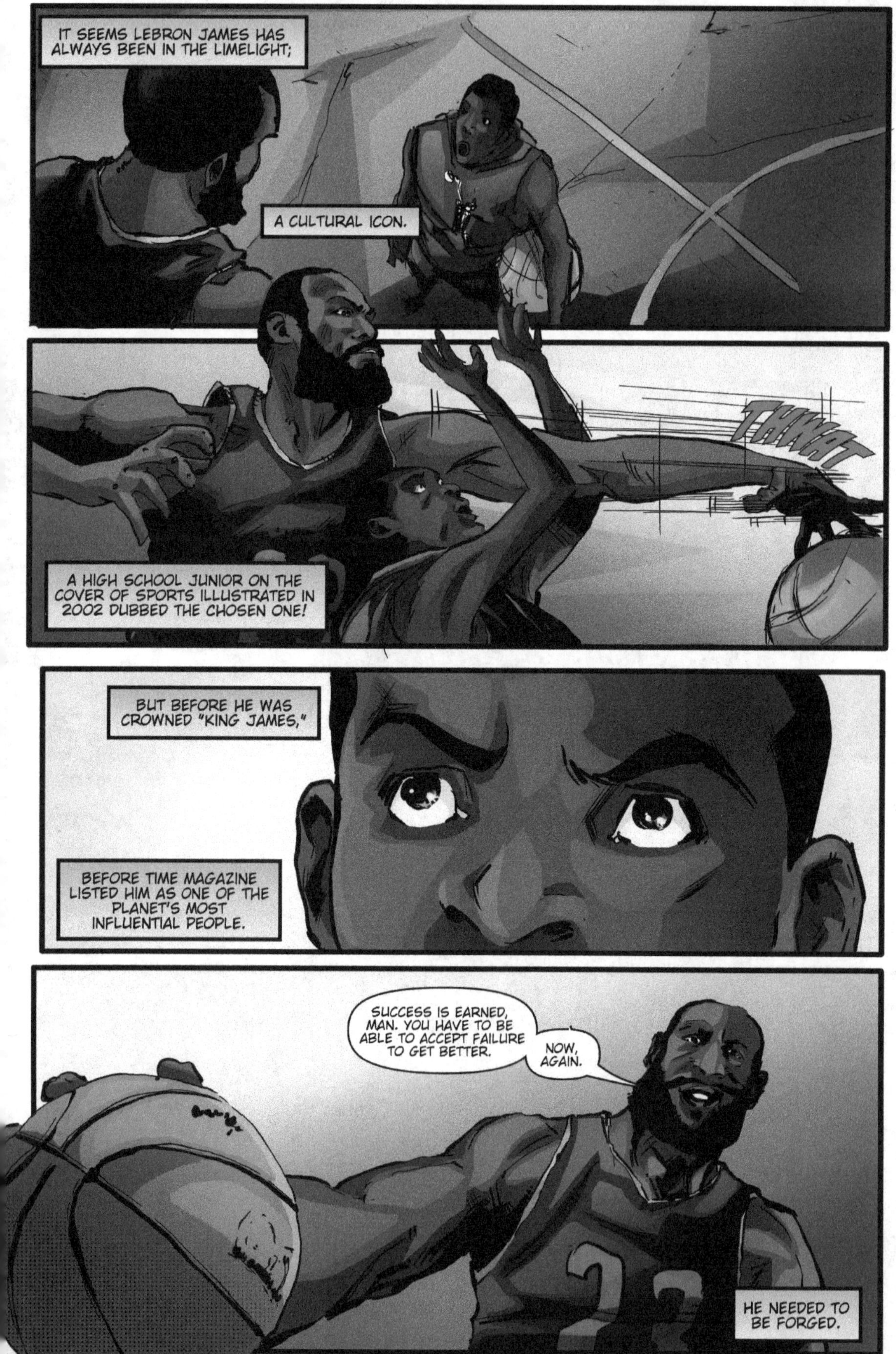
IT SEEMS LEBRON JAMES HAS ALWAYS BEEN IN THE LIMELIGHT;
A CULTURAL ICON.
THWAT
A HIGH SCHOOL JUNIOR ON THE COVER OF SPORTS ILLUSTRATED IN 2002 DUBBED THE CHOSEN ONE!
BUT BEFORE HE WAS CROWNED "KING JAMES,"
BEFORE TIME MAGAZINE LISTED HIM AS ONE OF THE PLANET'S MOST INFLUENTIAL PEOPLE.
SUCCESS IS EARNED, MAN. YOU HAVE TO BE ABLE TO ACCEPT FAILURE TO GET BETTER.
NOW, AGAIN.
HE NEEDED TO BE FORGED.

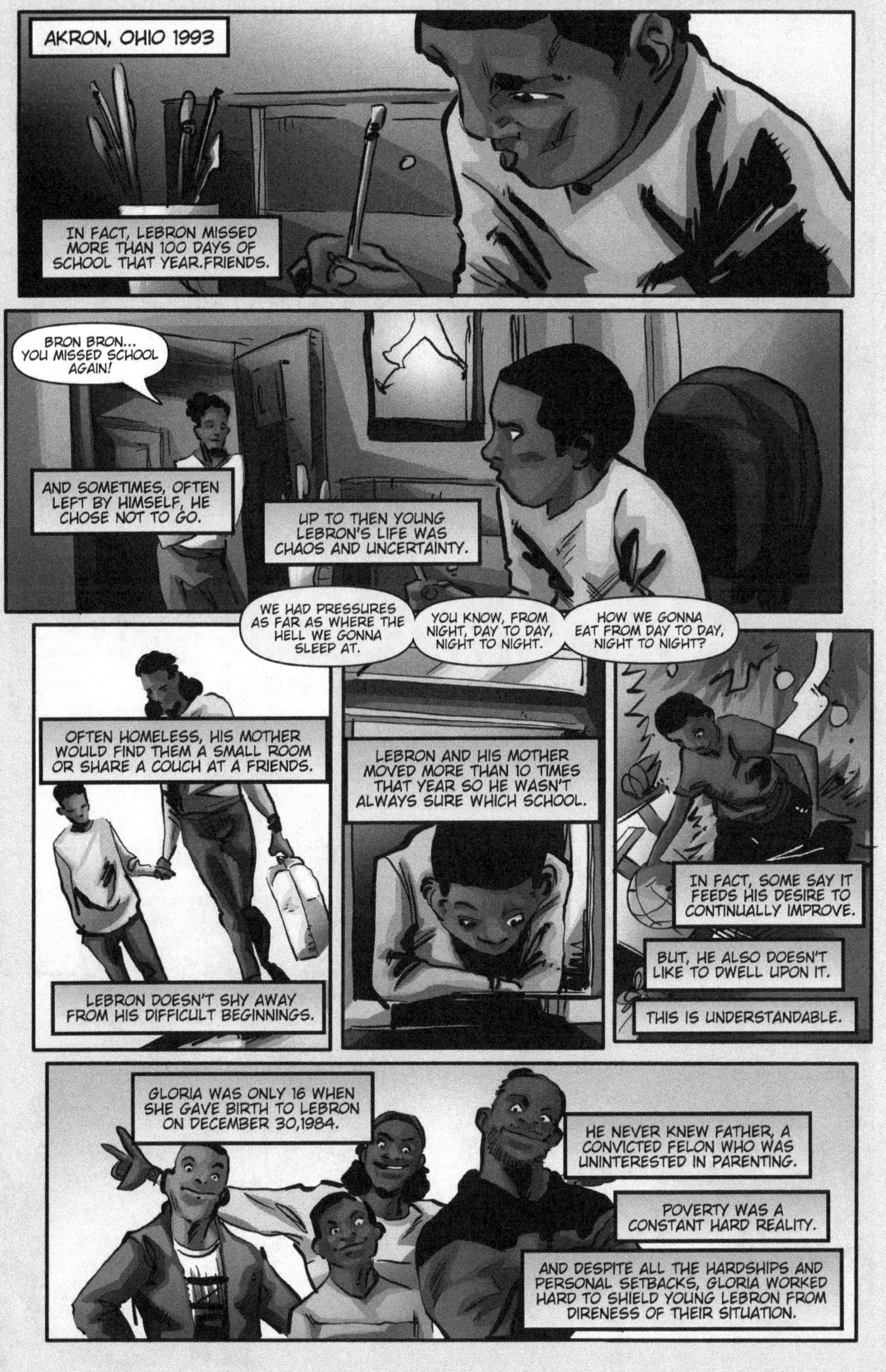
AKRON, OHIO 1993
IN FACT, LEBRON MISSED MORE THAN 100 DAYS OF SCHOOL THAT YEAR.FRIENDS.
BRON BRON... YOU MISSED SCHOOL AGAIN!
AND SOMETIMES, OFTEN LEFT BY HIMSELF, HE CHOSE NOT TO GO.
UP TO THEN YOUNG LEBRON'S LIFE WAS CHAOS AND UNCERTAINTY.
WE HAD PRESSURES AS FAR AS WHERE THE HELL WE GONNA SLEEP AT.
YOU KNOW, FROM NIGHT, DAY TO DAY, NIGHT TO NIGHT.
HOW WE GONNA EAT FROM DAY TO DAY, NIGHT TO NIGHT?
OFTEN HOMELESS, HIS MOTHER WOULD FIND THEM A SMALL ROOM OR SHARE A COUCH AT A FRIENDS.
LEBRON DOESN'T SHY AWAY FROM HIS DIFFICULT BEGINNINGS.
LEBRON AND HIS MOTHER MOVED MORE THAN 10 TIMES THAT YEAR SO HE WASN'T ALWAYS SURE WHICH SCHOOL.
IN FACT, SOME SAY IT FEEDS HIS DESIRE TO CONTINUALLY IMPROVE.
BUT, HE ALSO DOESN'T LIKE TO DWELL UPON IT.
THIS IS UNDERSTANDABLE.
GLORIA WAS ONLY 16 WHEN SHE GAVE BIRTH TO LEBRON ON DECEMBER 30,1984.
HE NEVER KNEW FATHER, A CONVICTED FELON WHO WAS UNINTERESTED IN PARENTING.
POVERTY WAS A CONSTANT HARD REALITY.
AND DESPITE ALL THE HARDSHIPS AND PERSONAL SETBACKS, GLORIA WORKED HARD TO SHIELD YOUNG LEBRON FROM DIRENESS OF THEIR SITUATION.

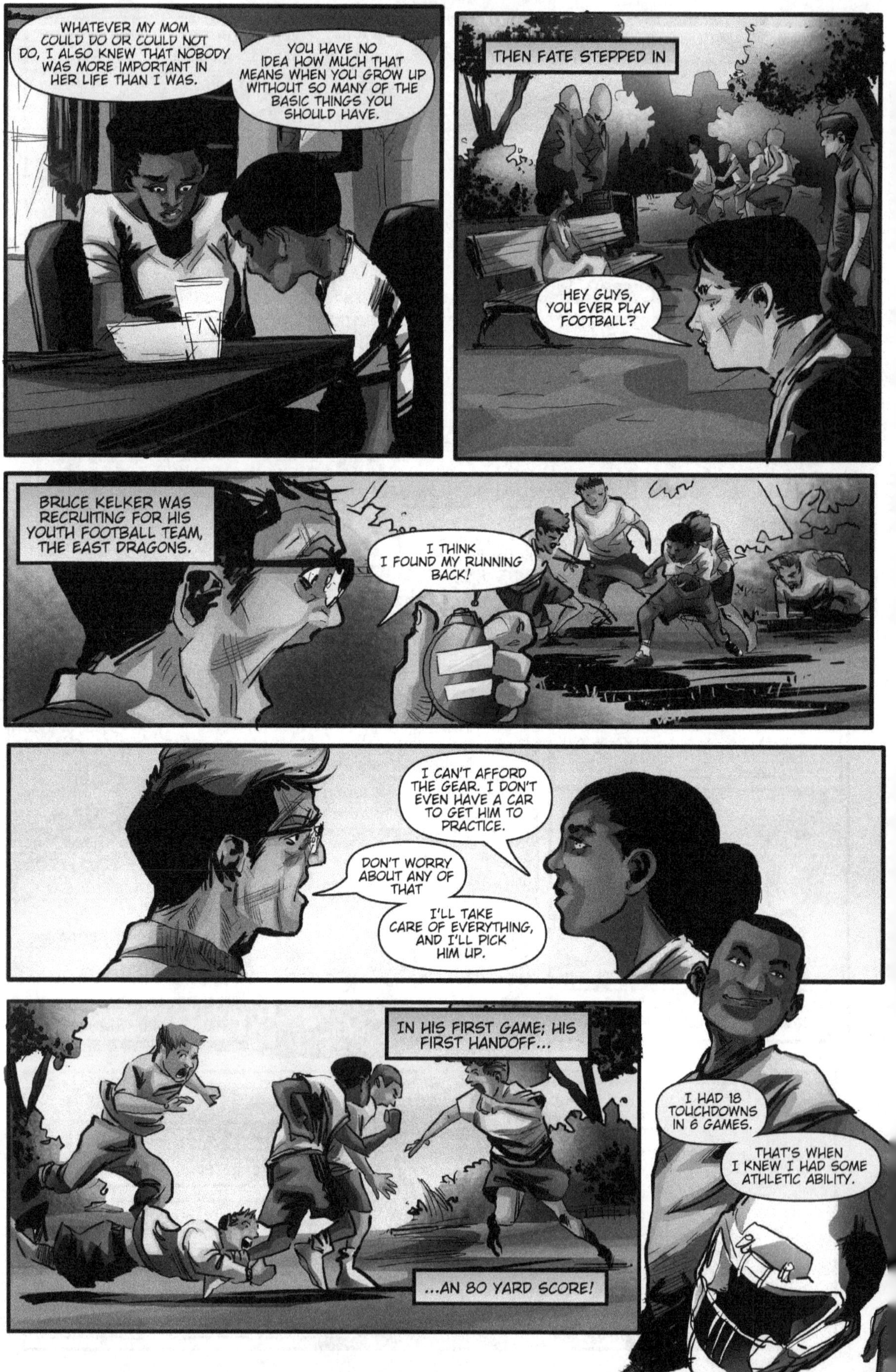
WHATEVER MY MOM COULD DO OR COULD NOT DO, I ALSO KNEW THAT NOBODY WAS MORE IMPORTANT IN HER LIFE THAN I WAS.
YOU HAVE NO IDEA HOW MUCH THAT MEANS WHEN YOU GROW UP WITHOUT SO MANY OF THE BASIC THINGS YOU SHOULD HAVE.
THEN FATE STEPPED IN
HEY GUYS, YOU EVER PLAY FOOTBALL?
BRUCE KELKER WAS RECRUITING FOR HIS YOUTH FOOTBALL TEAM, THE EAST DRAGONS.
I THINK I FOUND MY RUNNING BACK!
I CAN'T AFFORD THE GEAR. I DON'T EVEN HAVE A CAR TO GET HIM TO PRACTICE.
DON'T WORRY ABOUT ANY OF THAT
I'LL TAKE CARE OF EVERYTHING, AND I'LL PICK HIM UP.
IN HIS FIRST GAME; HIS FIRST HANDOFF...
...AN 80 YARD SCORE!
I HAD 18 TOUCHDOWNS IN 6 GAMES.
THAT'S WHEN I KNEW I HAD SOME ATHLETIC ABILITY.

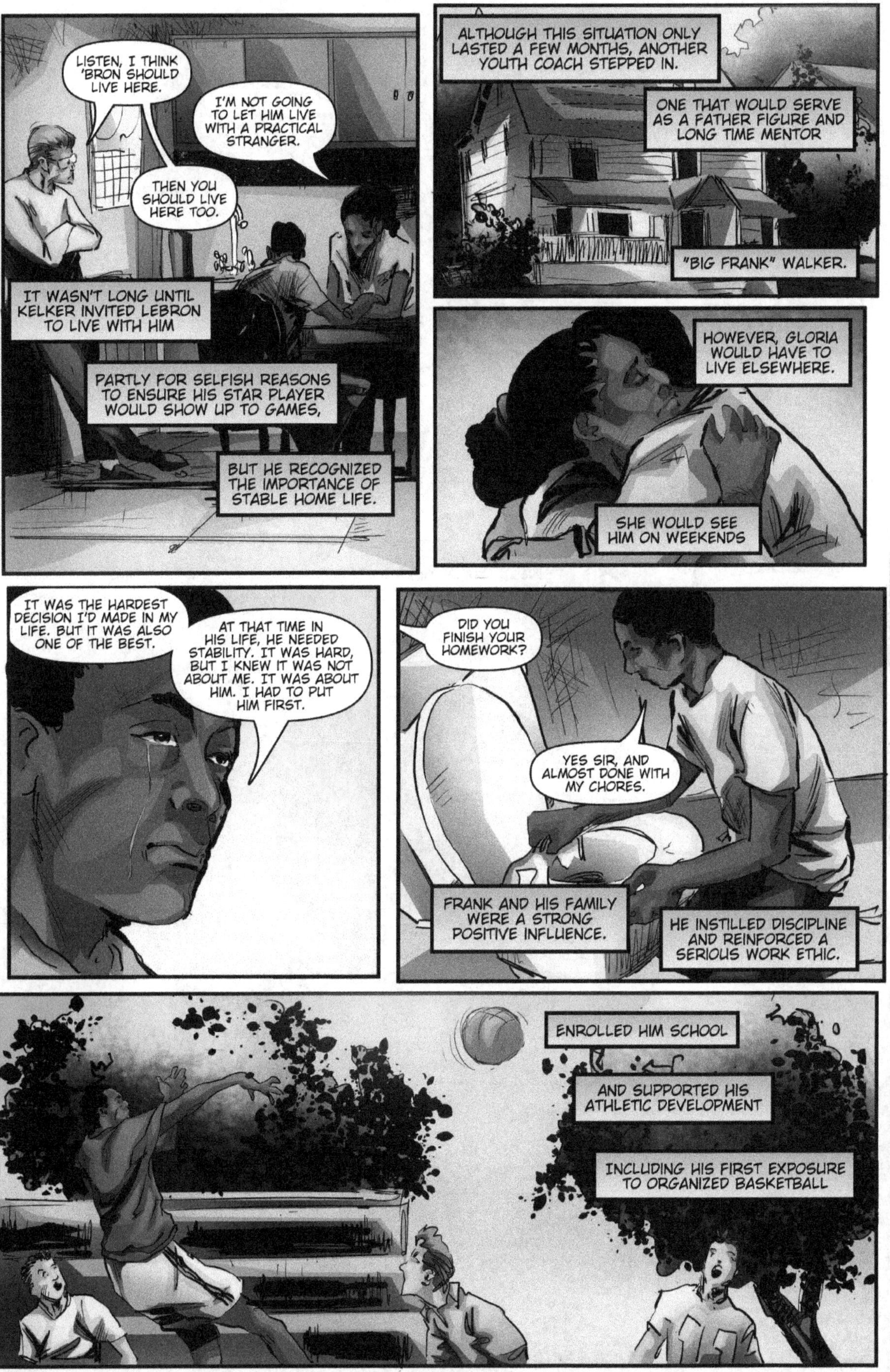
LISTEN, I THINK 'BRON SHOULD LIVE HERE.
I'M NOT GOING TO LET HIM LIVE WITH A PRACTICAL STRANGER.
THEN YOU SHOULD LIVE HERE TOO.
IT WASN'T LONG UNTIL KELKER INVITED LEBRON TO LIVE WITH HIM
PARTLY FOR SELFISH REASONS TO ENSURE HIS STAR PLAYER WOULD SHOW UP TO GAMES,
BUT HE RECOGNIZED THE IMPORTANCE OF STABLE HOME LIFE.
ALTHOUGH THIS SITUATION ONLY LASTED A FEW MONTHS, ANOTHER YOUTH COACH STEPPED IN.
ONE THAT WOULD SERVE AS A FATHER FIGURE AND LONG TIME MENTOR
"BIG FRANK" WALKER.
HOWEVER, GLORIA WOULD HAVE TO LIVE ELSEWHERE.
SHE WOULD SEE HIM ON WEEKENDS
IT WAS THE HARDEST DECISION I'D MADE IN MY LIFE. BUT IT WAS ALSO ONE OF THE BEST.
AT THAT TIME IN HIS LIFE, HE NEEDED STABILITY. IT WAS HARD, BUT I KNEW IT WAS NOT ABOUT ME. IT WAS ABOUT HIM. I HAD TO PUT HIM FIRST.
DID YOU FINISH YOUR HOMEWORK?
YES SIR, AND ALMOST DONE WITH MY CHORES.
FRANK AND HIS FAMILY WERE A STRONG POSITIVE INFLUENCE.
HE INSTILLED DISCIPLINE AND REINFORCED A SERIOUS WORK ETHIC.
ENROLLED HIM SCHOOL
AND SUPPORTED HIS ATHLETIC DEVELOPMENT
INCLUDING HIS FIRST EXPOSURE TO ORGANIZED BASKETBALL

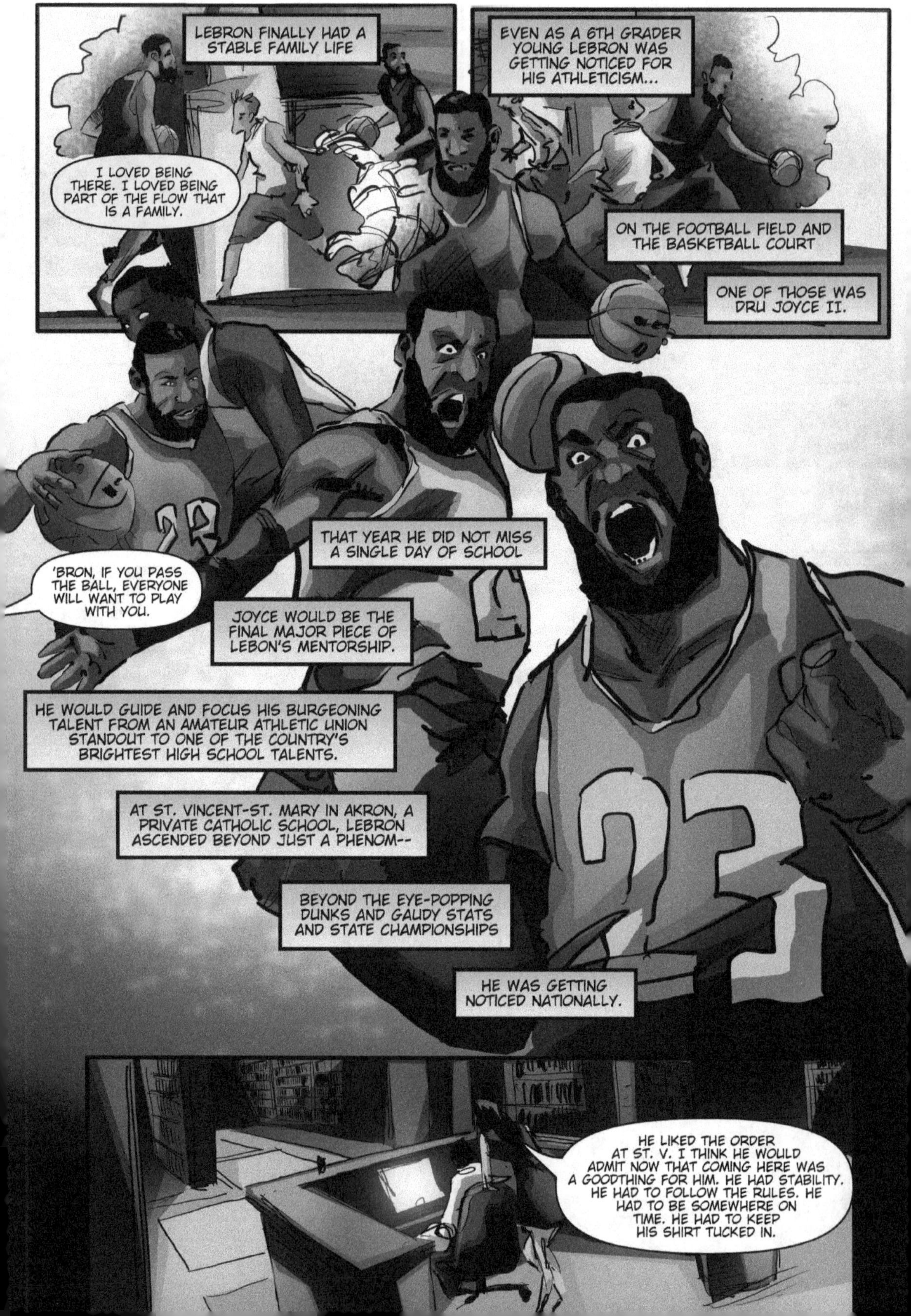
LEBRON FINALLY HAD A STABLE FAMILY LIFE
I LOVED BEING THERE. I LOVED BEING PART OF THE FLOW THAT IS A FAMILY.
EVEN AS A 6TH GRADER YOUNG LEBRON WAS GETTING NOTICED FOR HIS ATHLETICISM...
ON THE FOOTBALL FIELD AND THE BASKETBALL COURT
ONE OF THOSE WAS DRU JOYCE II.
THAT YEAR HE DID NOT MISS A SINGLE DAY OF SCHOOL
'BRON, IF YOU PASS THE BALL, EVERYONE WILL WANT TO PLAY WITH YOU.
JOYCE WOULD BE THE FINAL MAJOR PIECE OF LEBON'S MENTORSHIP.
HE WOULD GUIDE AND FOCUS HIS BURGEONING TALENT FROM AN AMATEUR ATHLETIC UNION STANDOUT TO ONE OF THE COUNTRY'S BRIGHTEST HIGH SCHOOL TALENTS.
AT ST. VINCENT-ST. MARY IN AKRON, A PRIVATE CATHOLIC SCHOOL, LEBRON ASCENDED BEYOND JUST A PHENOM--
BEYOND THE EYE-POPPING DUNKS AND GAUDY STATS AND STATE CHAMPIONSHIPS
HE WAS GETTING NOTICED NATIONALLY.
HE LIKED THE ORDER AT ST. V. I THINK HE WOULD ADMIT NOW THAT COMING HERE WAS A GOODTHING FOR HIM. HE HAD STABILITY. HE HAD TO FOLLOW THE RULES. HE HAD TO BE SOMEWHERE ON TIME. HE HAD TO KEEP HIS SHIRT TUCKED IN.

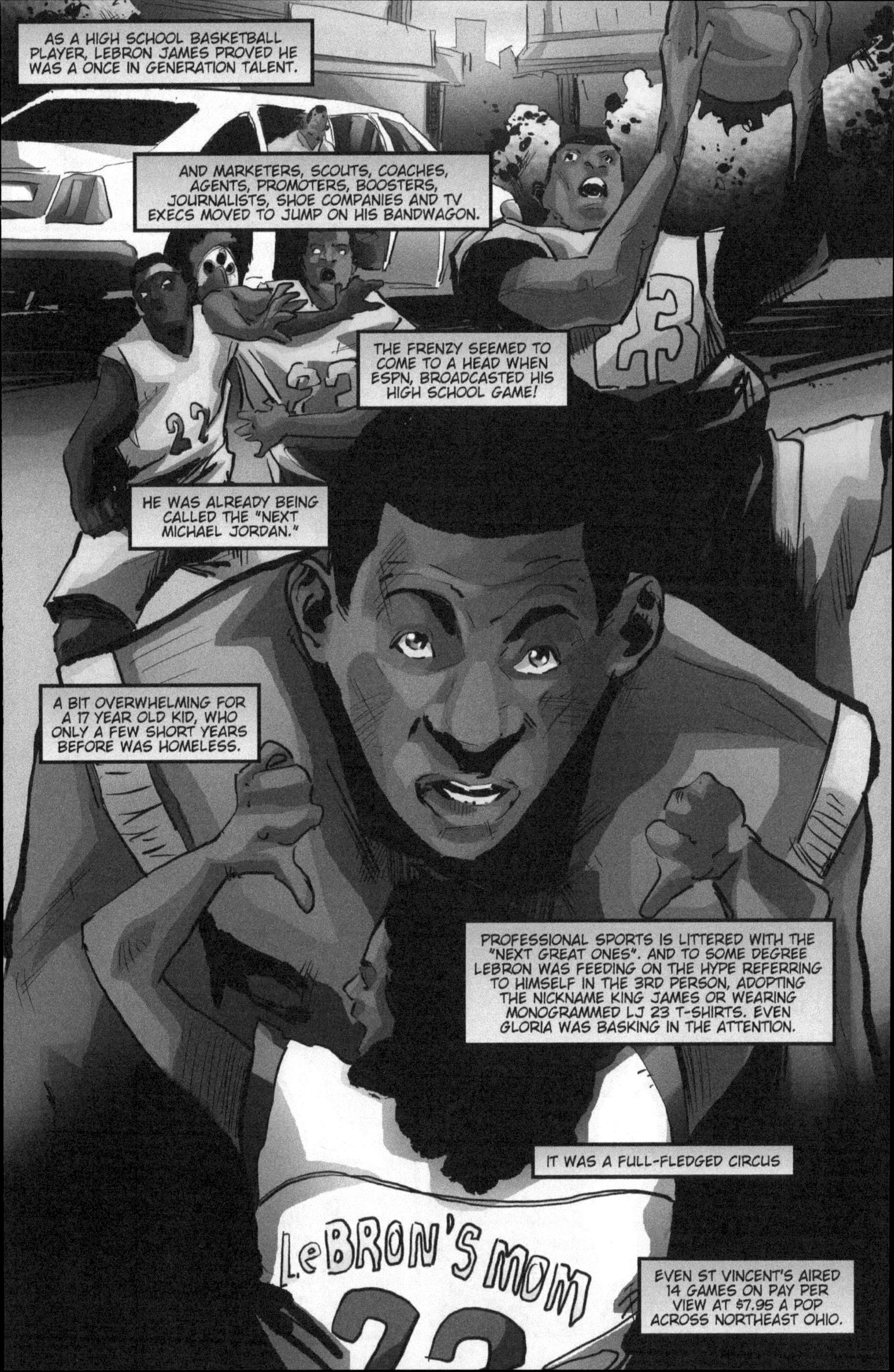
AS A HIGH SCHOOL BASKETBALL PLAYER, LEBRON JAMES PROVED HE WAS A ONCE IN GENERATION TALENT.
AND MARKETERS, SCOUTS, COACHES, AGENTS, PROMOTERS, BOOSTERS, JOURNALISTS, SHOE COMPANIES AND TV EXECS MOVED TO JUMP ON HIS BANDWAGON.
THE FRENZY SEEMED TO COME TO A HEAD WHEN ESPN, BROADCASTED HIS HIGH SCHOOL GAME!
HE WAS ALREADY BEING CALLED THE "NEXT MICHAEL JORDAN."
A BIT OVERWHELMING FOR A 17 YEAR OLD KID, WHO ONLY A FEW SHORT YEARS BEFORE WAS HOMELESS.
PROFESSIONAL SPORTS IS LITTERED WITH THE "NEXT GREAT ONES". AND TO SOME DEGREE LEBRON WAS FEEDING ON THE HYPE REFERRING TO HIMSELF IN THE 3RD PERSON, ADOPTING THE NICKNAME KING JAMES OR WEARING MONOGRAMMED LJ 23 T-SHIRTS. EVEN GLORIA WAS BASKING IN THE ATTENTION.
IT WAS A FULL-FLEDGED CIRCUS
LeBRON'S MOM
EVEN ST VINCENT'S AIRED 14 GAMES ON PAY PER VIEW AT $7.95 A POP ACROSS NORTHEAST OHIO.

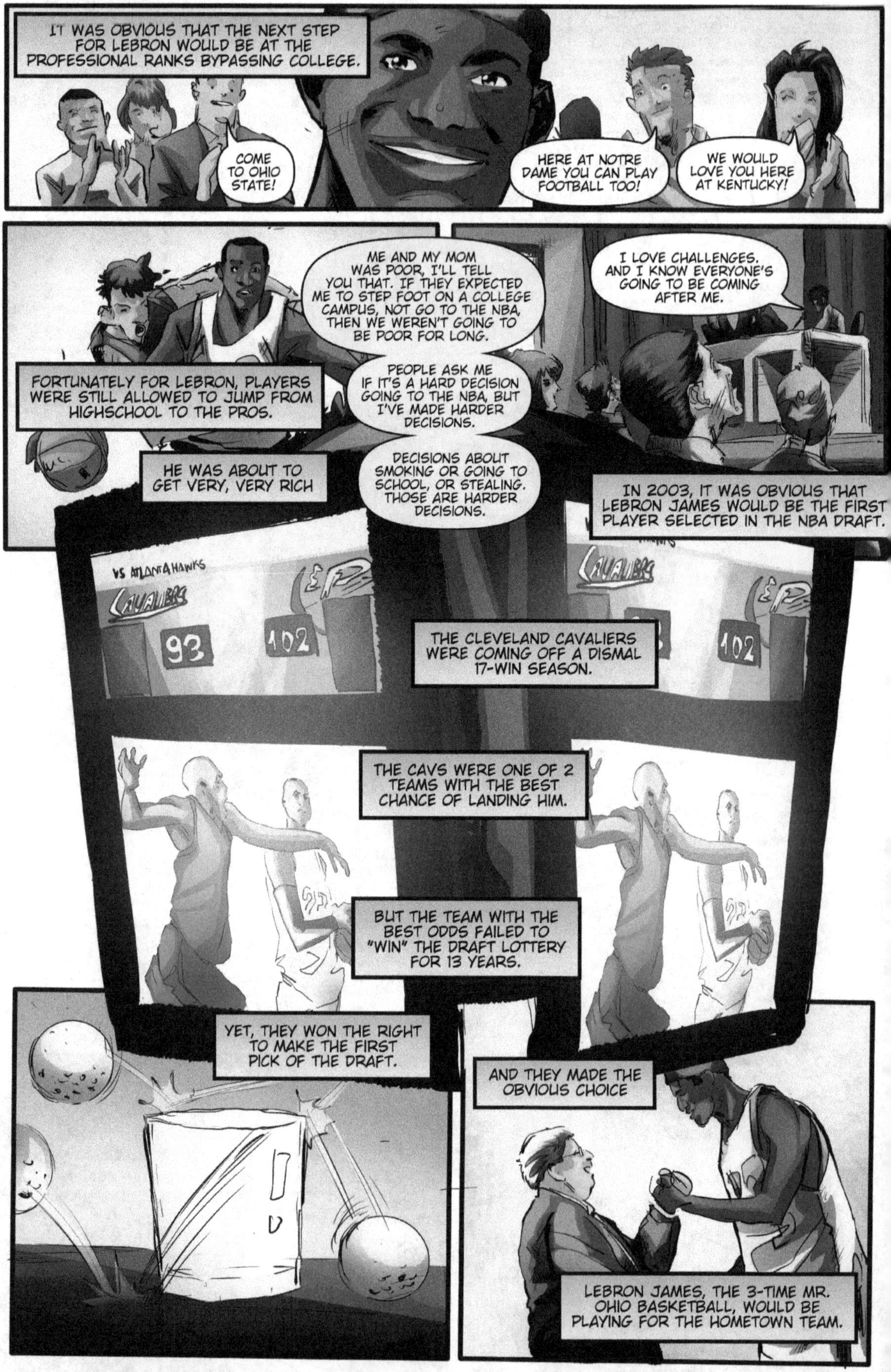
IT WAS OBVIOUS THAT THE NEXT STEP FOR LEBRON WOULD BE AT THE PROFESSIONAL RANKS BYPASSING COLLEGE.
COME TO OHIO STATE!
HERE AT NOTRE DAME YOU CAN PLAY FOOTBALL TOO!
WE WOULD LOVE YOU HERE AT KENTUCKY!
ME AND MY MOM WAS POOR, I'LL TELL YOU THAT. IF THEY EXPECTED ME TO STEP FOOT ON A COLLEGE CAMPUS, NOT GO TO THE NBA, THEN WE WEREN'T GOING TO BE POOR FOR LONG.
FORTUNATELY FOR LEBRON, PLAYERS WERE STILL ALLOWED TO JUMP FROM HIGHSCHOOL TO THE PROS.
PEOPLE ASK ME IF IT'S A HARD DECISION GOING TO THE NBA, BUT I'VE MADE HARDER DECISIONS.
HE WAS ABOUT TO GET VERY, VERY RICH
DECISIONS ABOUT SMOKING OR GOING TO SCHOOL, OR STEALING. THOSE ARE HARDER DECISIONS.
I LOVE CHALLENGES. AND I KNOW EVERYONE'S GOING TO BE COMING AFTER ME.
IN 2003, IT WAS OBVIOUS THAT LEBRON JAMES WOULD BE THE FIRST PLAYER SELECTED IN THE NBA DRAFT.
VS ATLANTA HAWKS
93
102
THE CLEVELAND CAVALIERS WERE COMING OFF A DISMAL 17-WIN SEASON.
102
THE CAVS WERE ONE OF 2 TEAMS WITH THE BEST CHANCE OF LANDING HIM.
BUT THE TEAM WITH THE BEST ODDS FAILED TO "WIN" THE DRAFT LOTTERY FOR 13 YEARS.
YET, THEY WON THE RIGHT TO MAKE THE FIRST PICK OF THE DRAFT.
AND THEY MADE THE OBVIOUS CHOICE
LEBRON JAMES, THE 3-TIME MR. OHIO BASKETBALL, WOULD BE PLAYING FOR THE HOMETOWN TEAM.

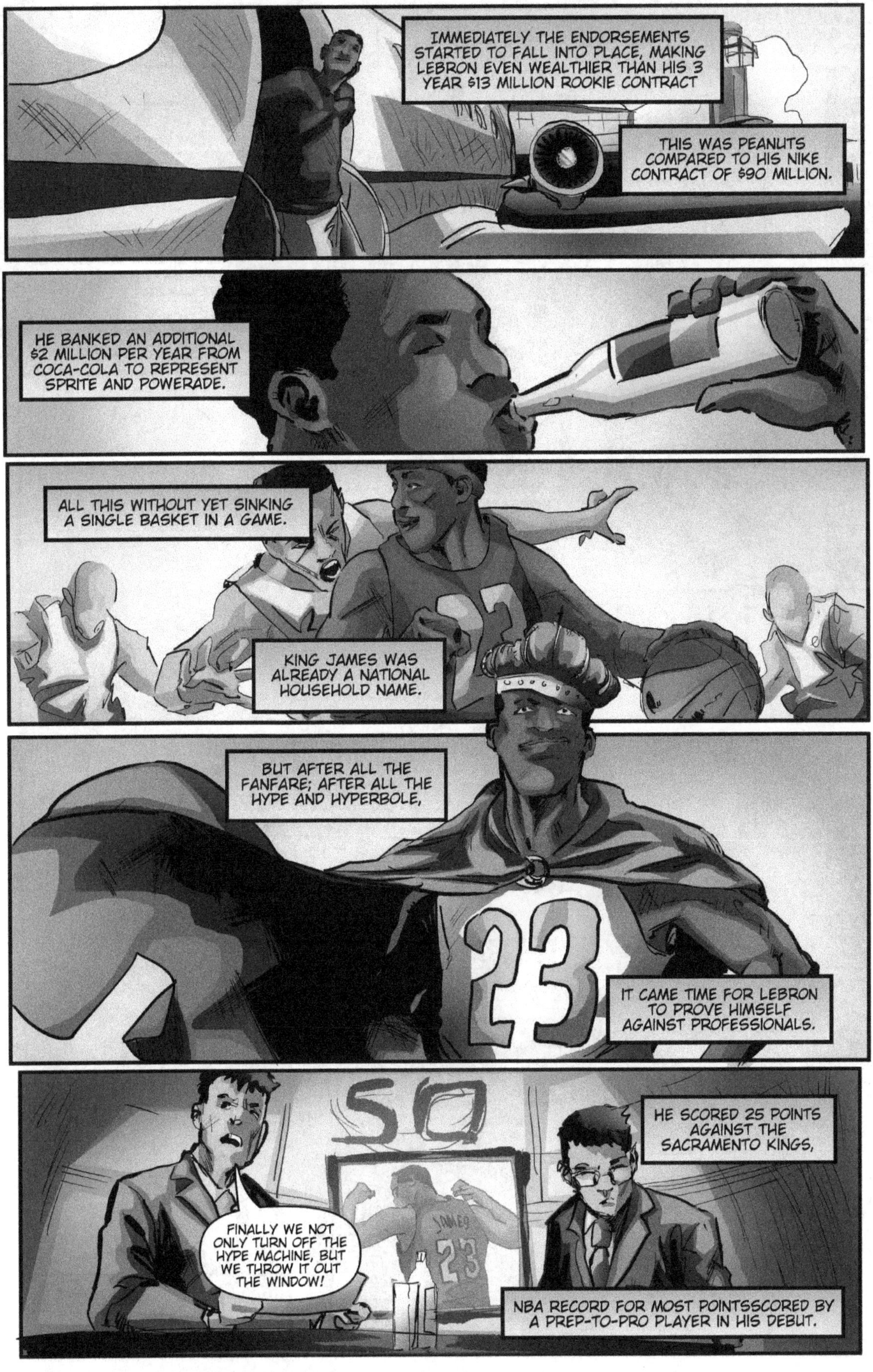
IMMEDIATELY THE ENDORSEMENTS STARTED TO FALL INTO PLACE, MAKING LEBRON EVEN WEALTHIER THAN HIS 3 YEAR $13 MILLION ROOKIE CONTRACT
THIS WAS PEANUTS COMPARED TO HIS NIKE CONTRACT OF $90 MILLION.
HE BANKED AN ADDITIONAL $2 MILLION PER YEAR FROM COCA-COLA TO REPRESENT SPRITE AND POWERADE.
ALL THIS WITHOUT YET SINKING A SINGLE BASKET IN A GAME.
KING JAMES WAS ALREADY A NATIONAL HOUSEHOLD NAME.
BUT AFTER ALL THE FANFARE; AFTER ALL THE HYPE AND HYPERBOLE,
IT CAME TIME FOR LEBRON TO PROVE HIMSELF AGAINST PROFESSIONALS.
HE SCORED 25 POINTS AGAINST THE SACRAMENTO KINGS,
FINALLY WE NOT ONLY TURN OFF THE HYPE MACHINE, BUT WE THROW IT OUT THE WINDOW!
NBA RECORD FOR MOST POINTSSCORED BY A PREP-TO-PRO PLAYER IN HIS DEBUT.

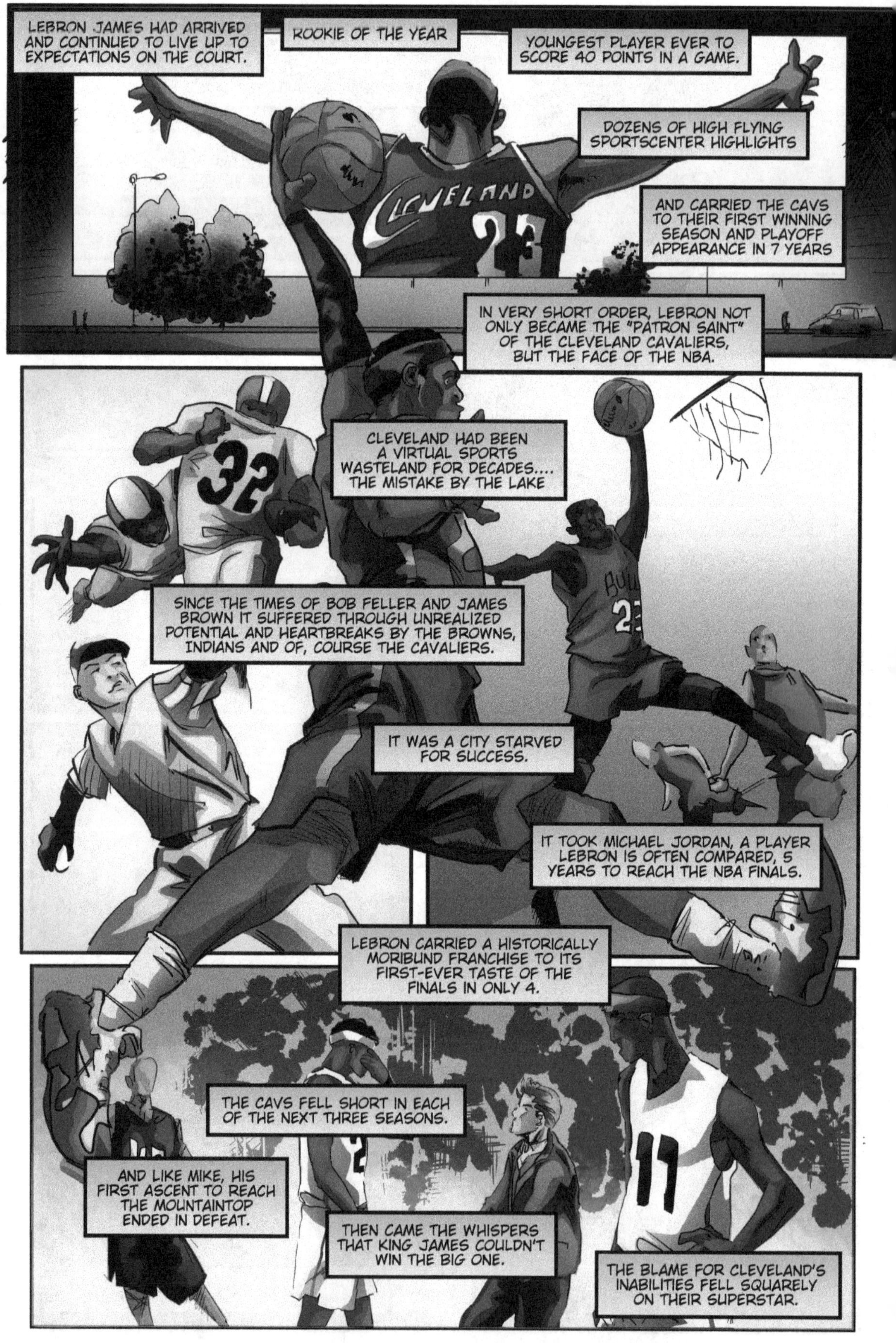
LEBRON JAMES HAD ARRIVED AND CONTINUED TO LIVE UP TO EXPECTATIONS ON THE COURT.
ROOKIE OF THE YEAR
YOUNGEST PLAYER EVER TO SCORE 40 POINTS IN A GAME.
DOZENS OF HIGH FLYING SPORTSCENTER HIGHLIGHTS
AND CARRIED THE CAVS TO THEIR FIRST WINNING SEASON AND PLAYOFF APPEARANCE IN 7 YEARS
CLEVELAND
23
IN VERY SHORT ORDER, LEBRON NOT ONLY BECAME THE "PATRON SAINT" OF THE CLEVELAND CAVALIERS, BUT THE FACE OF THE NBA.
CLEVELAND HAD BEEN A VIRTUAL SPORTS WASTELAND FOR DECADES.... THE MISTAKE BY THE LAKE
32
SINCE THE TIMES OF BOB FELLER AND JAMES BROWN IT SUFFERED THROUGH UNREALIZED POTENTIAL AND HEARTBREAKS BY THE BROWNS, INDIANS AND OF, COURSE THE CAVALIERS.
IT WAS A CITY STARVED FOR SUCCESS.
IT TOOK MICHAEL JORDAN, A PLAYER LEBRON IS OFTEN COMPARED, 5 YEARS TO REACH THE NBA FINALS.
LEBRON CARRIED A HISTORICALLY MORIBUND FRANCHISE TO ITS FIRST-EVER TASTE OF THE FINALS IN ONLY 4.
THE CAVS FELL SHORT IN EACH OF THE NEXT THREE SEASONS.
AND LIKE MIKE, HIS FIRST ASCENT TO REACH THE MOUNTAINTOP ENDED IN DEFEAT.
THEN CAME THE WHISPERS THAT KING JAMES COULDN'T WIN THE BIG ONE.
11
THE BLAME FOR CLEVELAND'S INABILITIES FELL SQUARELY ON THEIR SUPERSTAR.

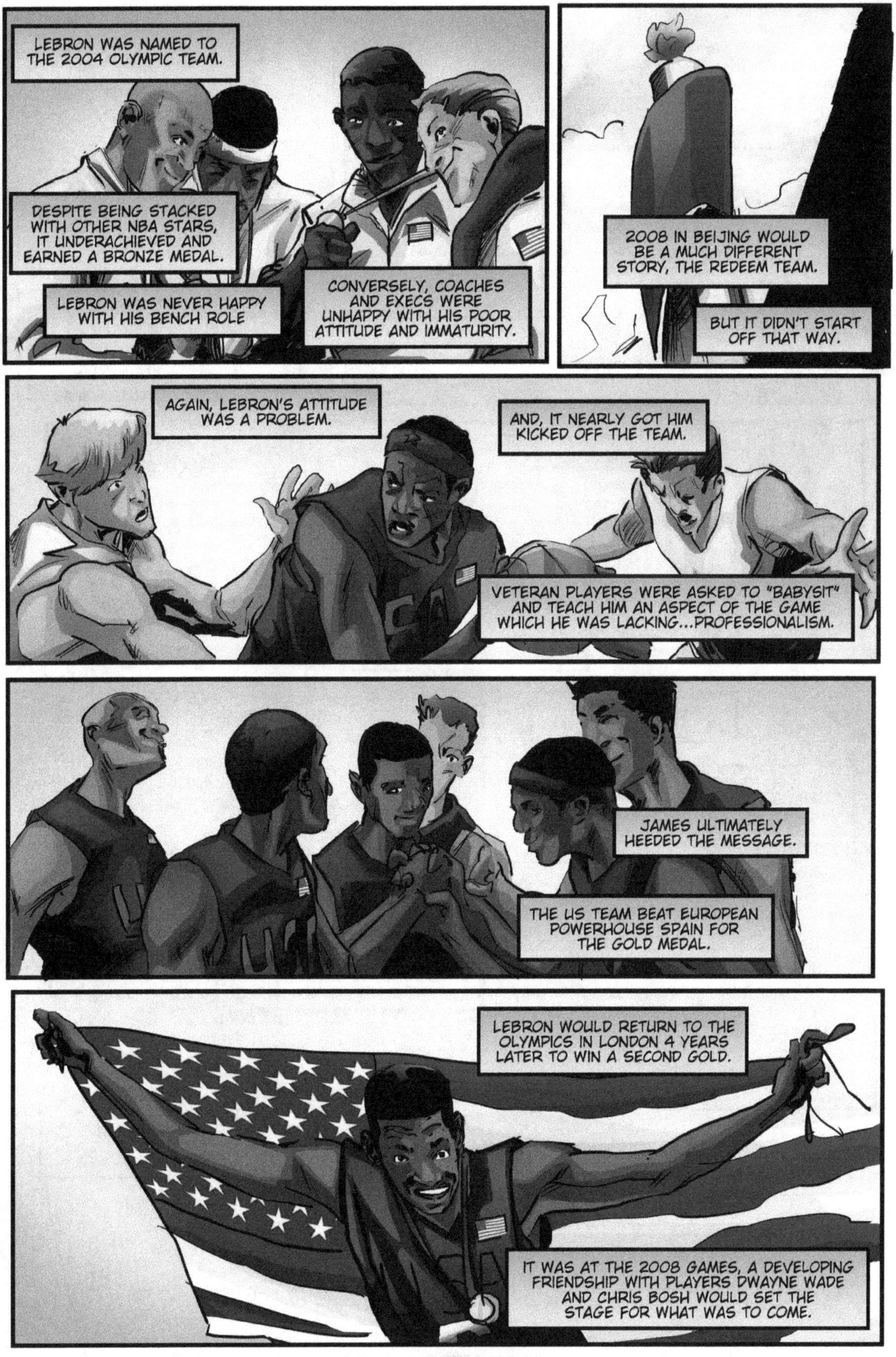
LEBRON WAS NAMED TO THE 2004 OLYMPIC TEAM.
DESPITE BEING STACKED WITH OTHER NBA STARS, IT UNDERACHIEVED AND EARNED A BRONZE MEDAL.
LEBRON WAS NEVER HAPPY WITH HIS BENCH ROLE
CONVERSELY, COACHES AND EXECS WERE UNHAPPY WITH HIS POOR ATTITUDE AND IMMATURITY.
2008 IN BEIJING WOULD BE A MUCH DIFFERENT STORY, THE REDEEM TEAM.
BUT IT DIDN'T START OFF THAT WAY.
AGAIN, LEBRON'S ATTITUDE WAS A PROBLEM.
AND, IT NEARLY GOT HIM KICKED OFF THE TEAM.
VETERAN PLAYERS WERE ASKED TO "BABYSIT" AND TEACH HIM AN ASPECT OF THE GAME WHICH HE WAS LACKING...PROFESSIONALISM.
JAMES ULTIMATELY HEEDED THE MESSAGE.
THE US TEAM BEAT EUROPEAN POWERHOUSE SPAIN FOR THE GOLD MEDAL.
LEBRON WOULD RETURN TO THE OLYMPICS IN LONDON 4 YEARS LATER TO WIN A SECOND GOLD.
IT WAS AT THE 2008 GAMES, A DEVELOPING FRIENDSHIP WITH PLAYERS DWAYNE WADE AND CHRIS BOSH WOULD SET THE STAGE FOR WHAT WAS TO COME.

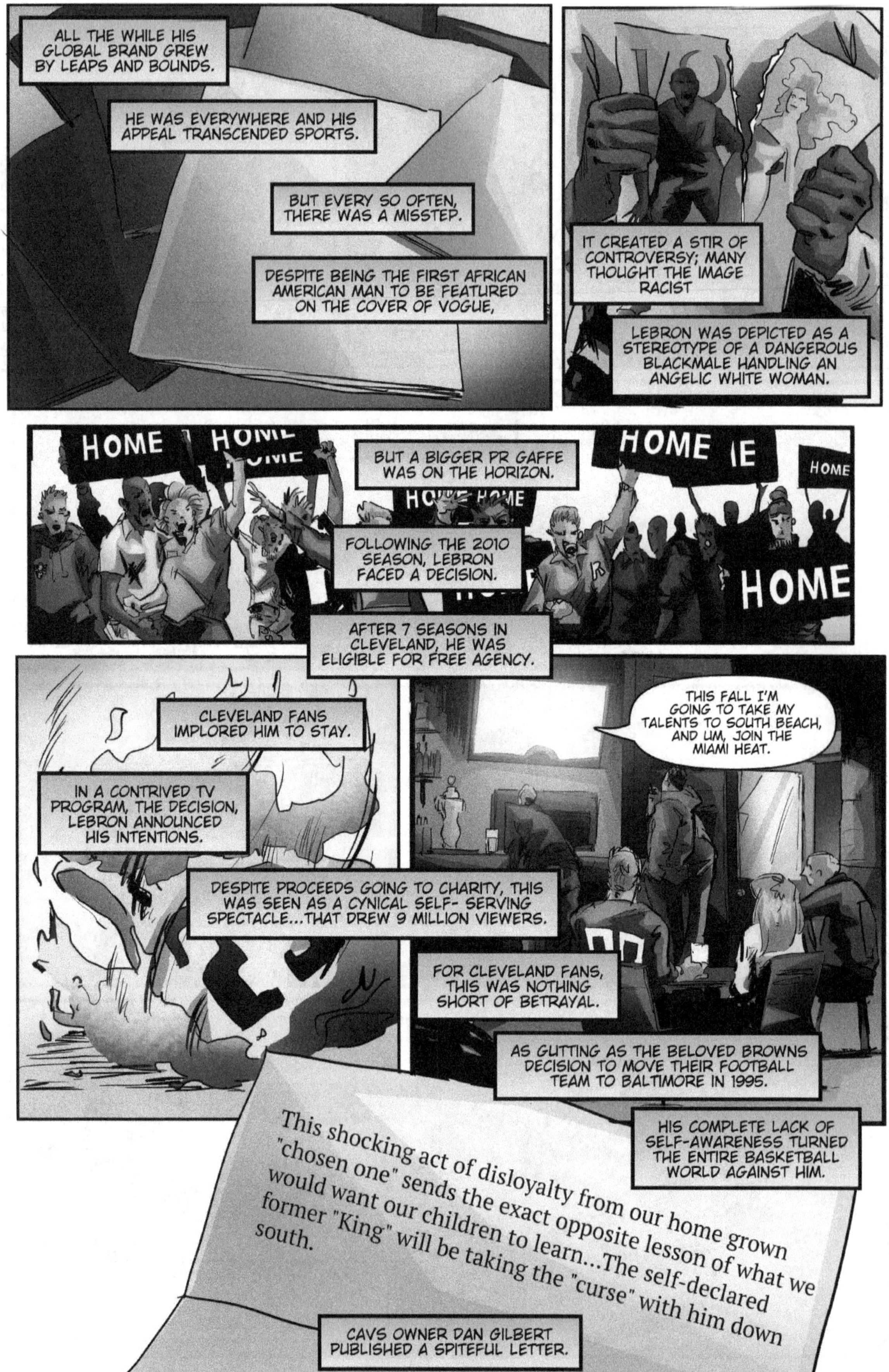
ALL THE WHILE HIS GLOBAL BRAND GREW BY LEAPS AND BOUNDS.
HE WAS EVERYWHERE AND HIS APPEAL TRANSCENDED SPORTS.
BUT EVERY SO OFTEN, THERE WAS A MISSTEP.
DESPITE BEING THE FIRST AFRICAN AMERICAN MAN TO BE FEATURED ON THE COVER OF VOGUE,
IT CREATED A STIR OF CONTROVERSY; MANY THOUGHT THE IMAGE RACIST
LEBRON WAS DEPICTED AS A STEREOTYPE OF A DANGEROUS BLACKMALE HANDLING AN ANGELIC WHITE WOMAN.
HOME
HOME
BUT A BIGGER PR GAFFE WAS ON THE HORIZON.
HOME
HOME
FOLLOWING THE 2010 SEASON, LEBRON FACED A DECISION.
HOME
AFTER 7 SEASONS IN CLEVELAND, HE WAS ELIGIBLE FOR FREE AGENCY.
CLEVELAND FANS IMPLORED HIM TO STAY.
IN A CONTRIVED TV PROGRAM, THE DECISION, LEBRON ANNOUNCED HIS INTENTIONS.
THIS FALL I'M GOING TO TAKE MY TALENTS TO SOUTH BEACH, AND UM, JOIN THE MIAMI HEAT.
DESPITE PROCEEDS GOING TO CHARITY, THIS WAS SEEN AS A CYNICAL SELF- SERVING SPECTACLE...THAT DREW 9 MILLION VIEWERS.
FOR CLEVELAND FANS, THIS WAS NOTHING SHORT OF BETRAYAL.
AS GUTTING AS THE BELOVED BROWNS DECISION TO MOVE THEIR FOOTBALL TEAM TO BALTIMORE IN 1995.
HIS COMPLETE LACK OF SELF-AWARENESS TURNED THE ENTIRE BASKETBALL WORLD AGAINST HIM.
This shocking act of disloyalty from our home grown "chosen one" sends the exact opposite lesson of what we would want our children to learn...The self-declared former "King" will be taking the "curse" with him down south.
CAVS OWNER DAN GILBERT PUBLISHED A SPITEFUL LETTER.

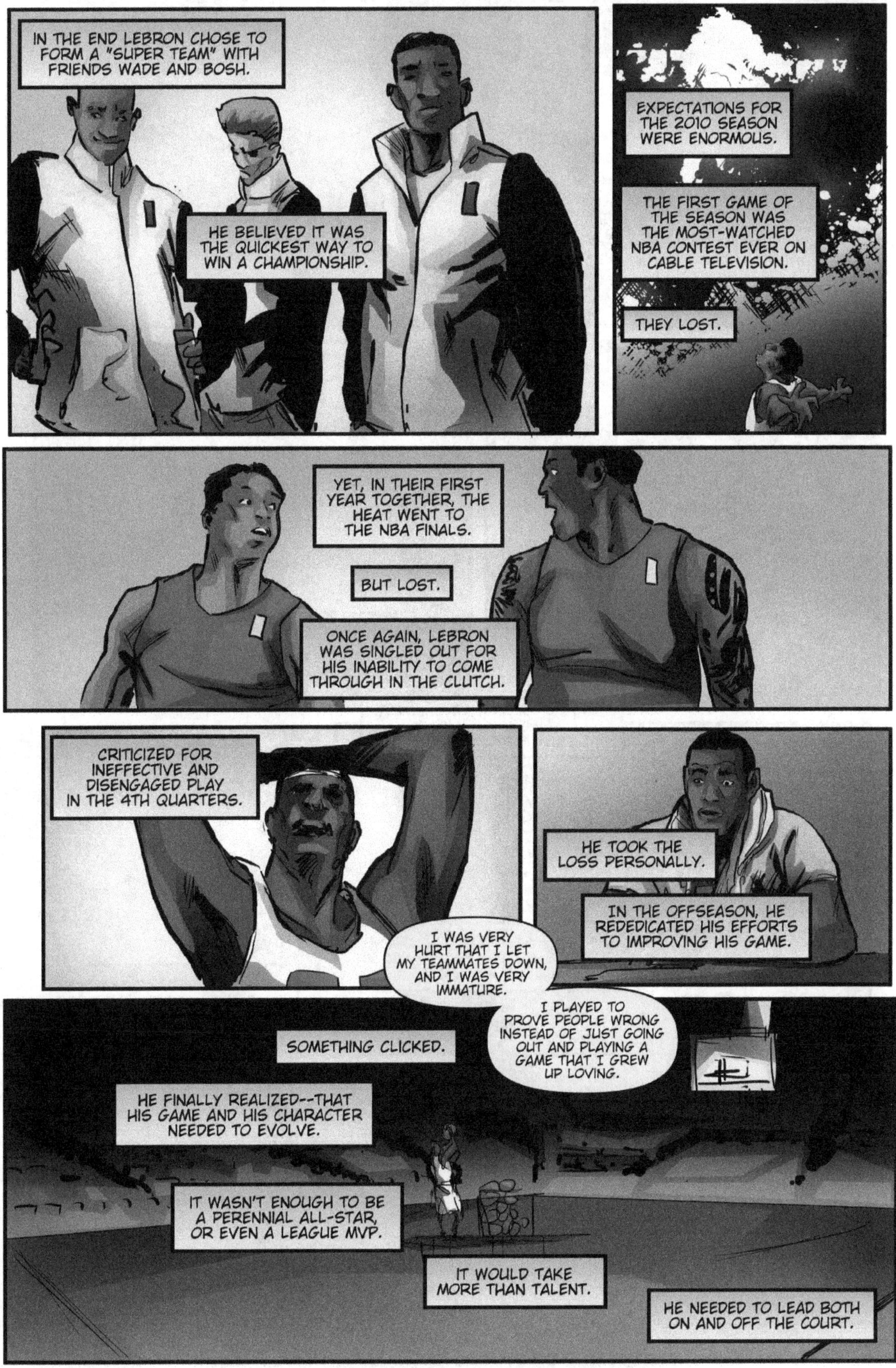

IN THE END LEBRON CHOSE TO FORM A "SUPER TEAM" WITH FRIENDS WADE AND BOSH.
HE BELIEVED IT WAS THE QUICKEST WAY TO WIN A CHAMPIONSHIP.
EXPECTATIONS FOR THE 2010 SEASON WERE ENORMOUS.
THE FIRST GAME OF THE SEASON WAS THE MOST-WATCHED NBA CONTEST EVER ON CABLE TELEVISION.
THEY LOST.
YET, IN THEIR FIRST YEAR TOGETHER, THE HEAT WENT TO THE NBA FINALS.
BUT LOST.
ONCE AGAIN, LEBRON WAS SINGLED OUT FOR HIS INABILITY TO COME THROUGH IN THE CLUTCH.
CRITICIZED FOR INEFFECTIVE AND DISENGAGED PLAY IN THE 4TH QUARTERS.
HE TOOK THE LOSS PERSONALLY.
IN THE OFFSEASON, HE REDEDICATED HIS EFFORTS TO IMPROVING HIS GAME.
I WAS VERY HURT THAT I LET MY TEAMMATES DOWN, AND I WAS VERY IMMATURE.
I PLAYED TO PROVE PEOPLE WRONG INSTEAD OF JUST GOING OUT AND PLAYING A GAME THAT I GREW UP LOVING.
SOMETHING CLICKED.
HE FINALLY REALIZED--THAT HIS GAME AND HIS CHARACTER NEEDED TO EVOLVE.
IT WASN'T ENOUGH TO BE A PERENNIAL ALL-STAR, OR EVEN A LEAGUE MVP.
IT WOULD TAKE MORE THAN TALENT.
HE NEEDED TO LEAD BOTH ON AND OFF THE COURT.

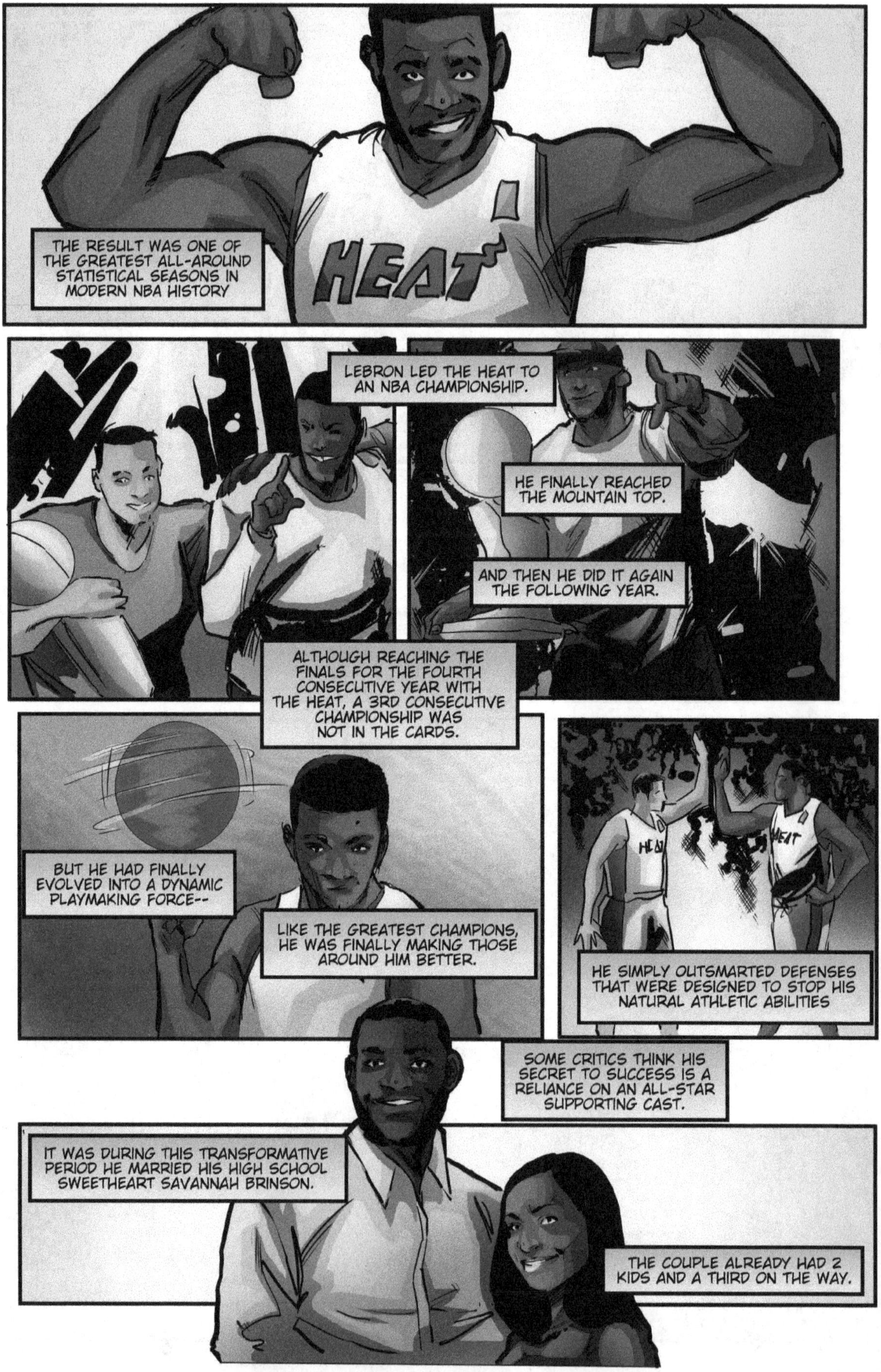
THE RESULT WAS ONE OF THE GREATEST ALL-AROUND STATISTICAL SEASONS IN MODERN NBA HISTORY
HEAT
LEBRON LED THE HEAT TO AN NBA CHAMPIONSHIP.
HE FINALLY REACHED THE MOUNTAIN TOP.
AND THEN HE DID IT AGAIN THE FOLLOWING YEAR.
ALTHOUGH REACHING THE FINALS FOR THE FOURTH CONSECUTIVE YEAR WITH THE HEAT, A 3RD CONSECUTIVE CHAMPIONSHIP WAS NOT IN THE CARDS.
BUT HE HAD FINALLY EVOLVED INTO A DYNAMIC PLAYMAKING FORCE--
LIKE THE GREATEST CHAMPIONS, HE WAS FINALLY MAKING THOSE AROUND HIM BETTER.
HE SIMPLY OUTSMARTED DEFENSES THAT WERE DESIGNED TO STOP HIS NATURAL ATHLETIC ABILITIES
SOME CRITICS THINK HIS SECRET TO SUCCESS IS A RELIANCE ON AN ALL-STAR SUPPORTING CAST.
IT WAS DURING THIS TRANSFORMATIVE PERIOD HE MARRIED HIS HIGH SCHOOL SWEETHEART SAVANNAH BRINSON.
THE COUPLE ALREADY HAD 2 KIDS AND A THIRD ON THE WAY.

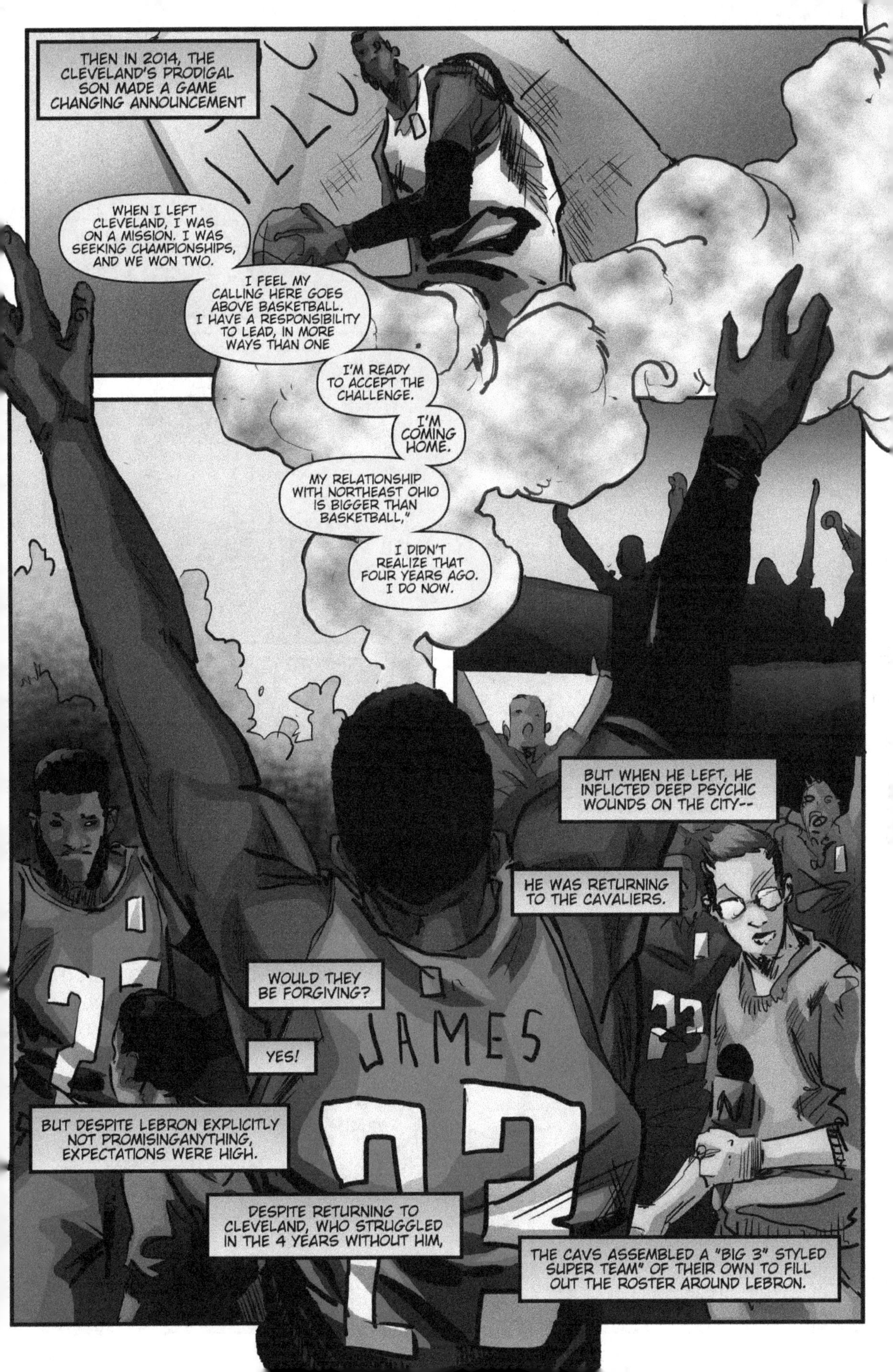
THEN IN 2014, THE CLEVELAND'S PRODIGAL SON MADE A GAME CHANGING ANNOUNCEMENT
WHEN I LEFT CLEVELAND, I WAS ON A MISSION. I WAS SEEKING CHAMPIONSHIPS, AND WE WON TWO.
I FEEL MY CALLING HERE GOES ABOVE BASKETBALL. I HAVE A RESPONSIBILITY TO LEAD, IN MORE WAYS THAN ONE
I'M READY TO ACCEPT THE CHALLENGE.
I'M COMING HOME.
MY RELATIONSHIP WITH NORTHEAST OHIO IS BIGGER THAN BASKETBALL,"
I DIDN'T REALIZE THAT FOUR YEARS AGO. I DO NOW.
BUT WHEN HE LEFT, HE INFLICTED DEEP PSYCHIC WOUNDS ON THE CITY--
HE WAS RETURNING TO THE CAVALIERS.
WOULD THEY BE FORGIVING?
JAMES
YES!
BUT DESPITE LEBRON EXPLICITLY NOT PROMISINGANYTHING, EXPECTATIONS WERE HIGH.
DESPITE RETURNING TO CLEVELAND, WHO STRUGGLED IN THE 4 YEARS WITHOUT HIM,
THE CAVS ASSEMBLED A "BIG 3" STYLED SUPER TEAM" OF THEIR OWN TO FILL OUT THE ROSTER AROUND LEBRON.

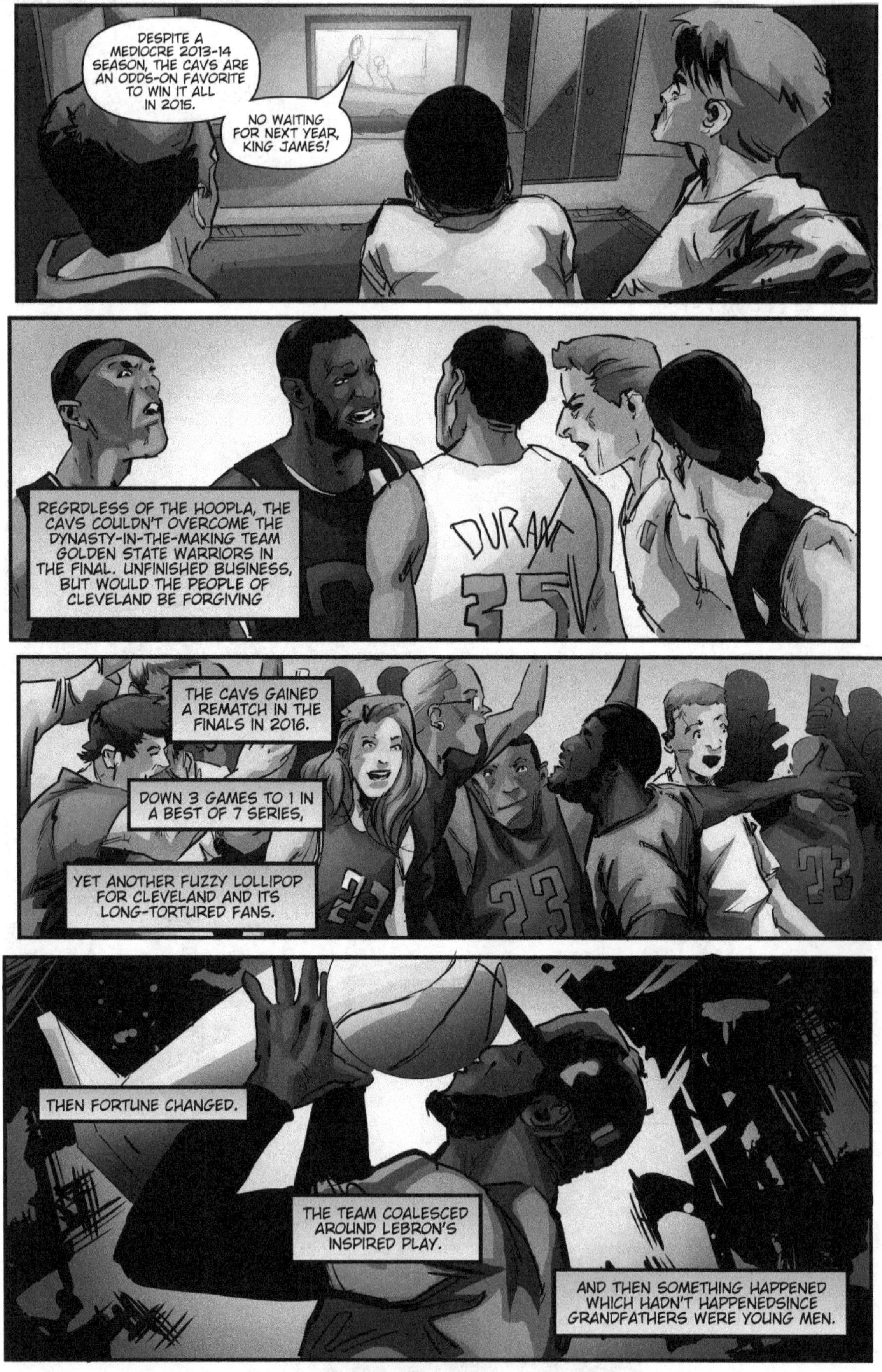
DESPITE A MEDIOCRE 2013-14 SEASON, THE CAVS ARE AN ODDS-ON FAVORITE TO WIN IT ALL IN 2015.
NO WAITING FOR NEXT YEAR, KING JAMES!
REGRDLESS OF THE HOOPLA, THE CAVS COULDN'T OVERCOME THE DYNASTY-IN-THE-MAKING TEAM GOLDEN STATE WARRIORS IN THE FINAL. UNFINISHED BUSINESS, BUT WOULD THE PEOPLE OF CLEVELAND BE FORGIVING
DURANT
35
THE CAVS GAINED A REMATCH IN THE FINALS IN 2016.
DOWN 3 GAMES TO 1 IN A BEST OF 7 SERIES,
YET ANOTHER FUZZY LOLLIPOP FOR CLEVELAND AND ITS LONG-TORTURED FANS.
23
THEN FORTUNE CHANGED.
THE TEAM COALESCED AROUND LEBRON'S INSPIRED PLAY.
AND THEN SOMETHING HAPPENED WHICH HADN'T HAPPENEDSINCE GRANDFATHERS WERE YOUNG MEN.

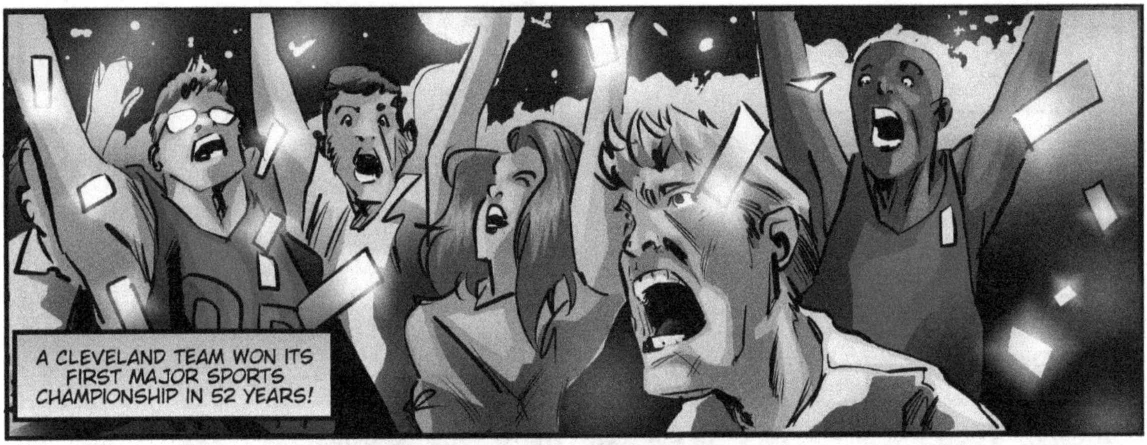
A CLEVELAND TEAM WON ITS FIRST MAJOR SPORTS CHAMPIONSHIP IN 52 YEARS!

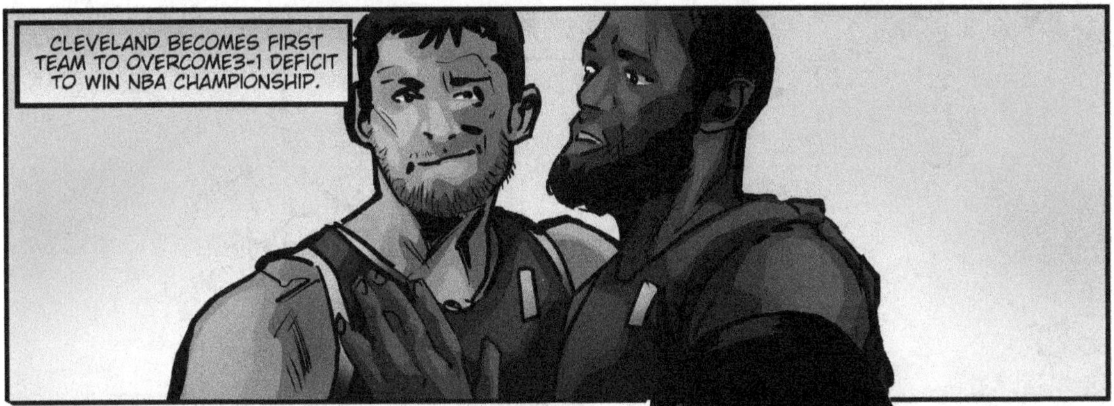
CLEVELAND BECOMES FIRST TEAM TO OVERCOME3-1 DEFICIT TO WIN NBA CHAMPIONSHIP.

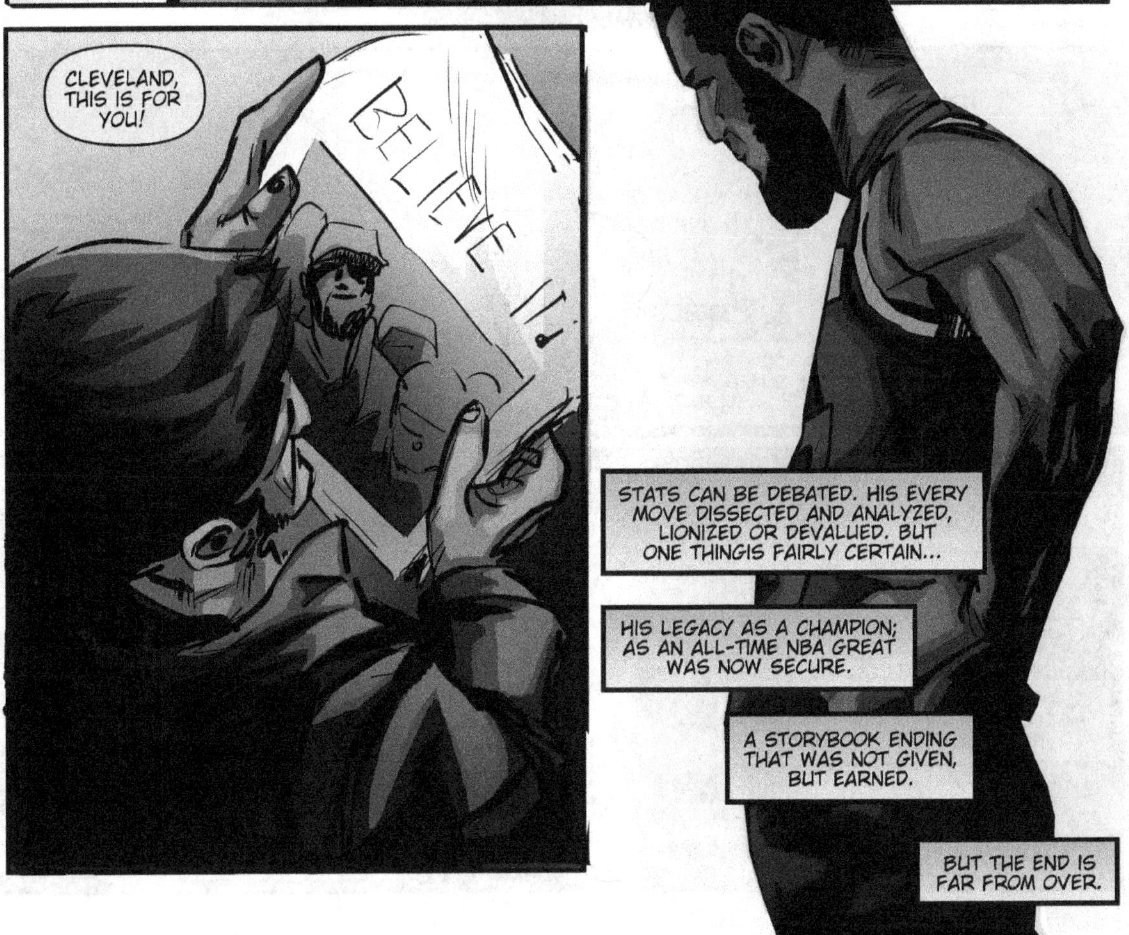
CLEVELAND, THIS IS FOR YOU!
BELIEVE IT!
STATS CAN BE DEBATED. HIS EVERY MOVE DISSECTED AND ANALYZED, LIONIZED OR DEVALUED. BUT ONE THINGIS FAIRLY CERTAIN...
HIS LEGACY AS A CHAMPION; AS AN ALL-TIME NBA GREAT WAS NOW SECURE.
A STORYBOOK ENDING THAT WAS NOT GIVEN, BUT EARNED.
BUT THE END IS FAR FROM OVER.

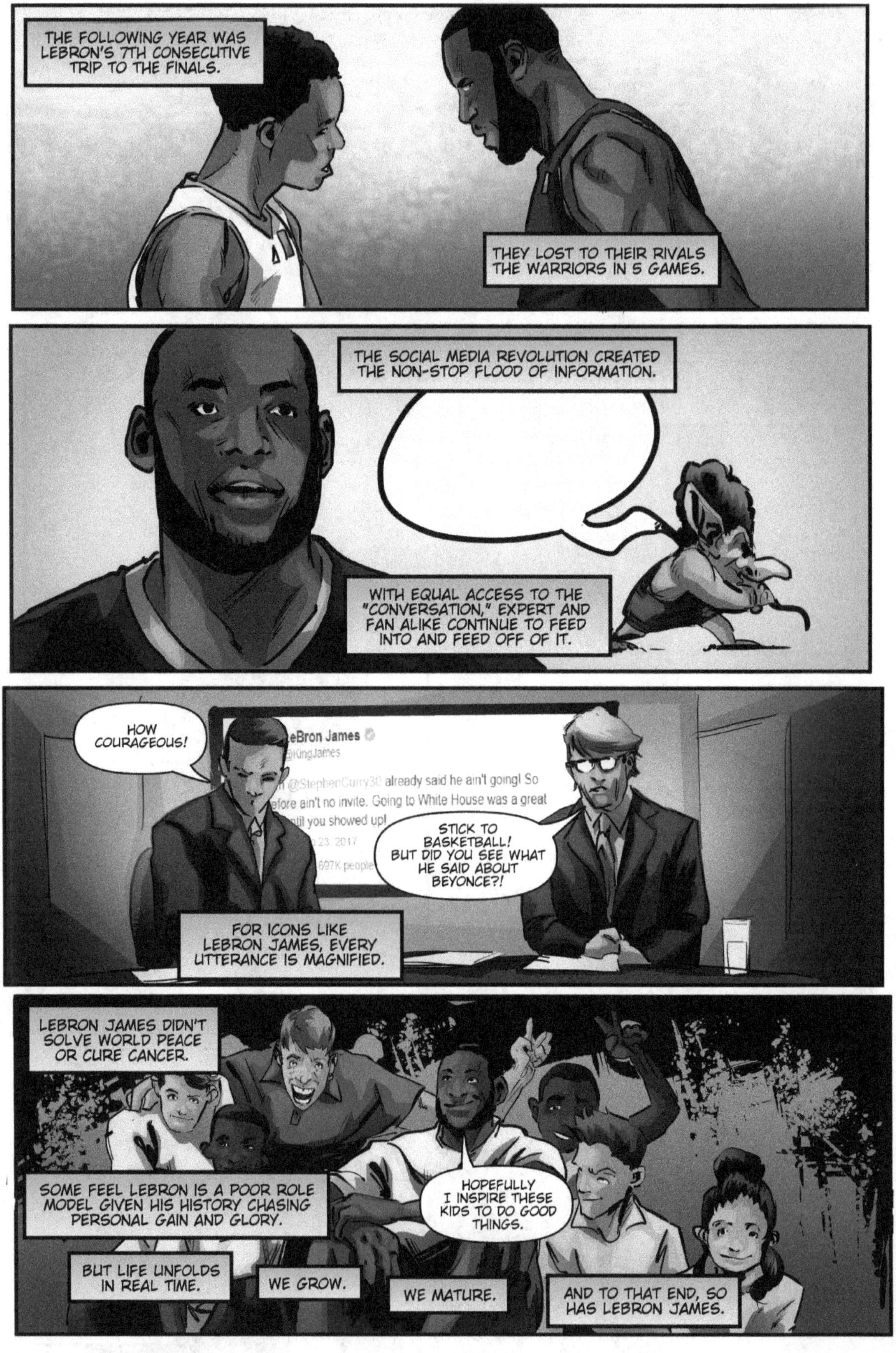
THE FOLLOWING YEAR WAS LEBRON'S 7TH CONSECUTIVE TRIP TO THE FINALS.
THEY LOST TO THEIR RIVALS THE WARRIORS IN 5 GAMES.
THE SOCIAL MEDIA REVOLUTION CREATED THE NON-STOP FLOOD OF INFORMATION.
WITH EQUAL ACCESS TO THE "CONVERSATION," EXPERT AND FAN ALIKE CONTINUE TO FEED INTO AND FEED OFF OF IT.
HOW COURAGEOUS!
STICK TO BASKETBALL! BUT DID YOU SEE WHAT HE SAID ABOUT BEYONCE?!
FOR ICONS LIKE LEBRON JAMES, EVERY UTTERANCE IS MAGNIFIED.
LEBRON JAMES DIDN'T SOLVE WORLD PEACE OR CURE CANCER.
SOME FEEL LEBRON IS A POOR ROLE MODEL GIVEN HIS HISTORY CHASING PERSONAL GAIN AND GLORY.
HOPEFULLY I INSPIRE THESE KIDS TO DO GOOD THINGS.
BUT LIFE UNFOLDS IN REAL TIME.
WE GROW.
WE MATURE.
AND TO THAT END, SO HAS LEBRON JAMES.

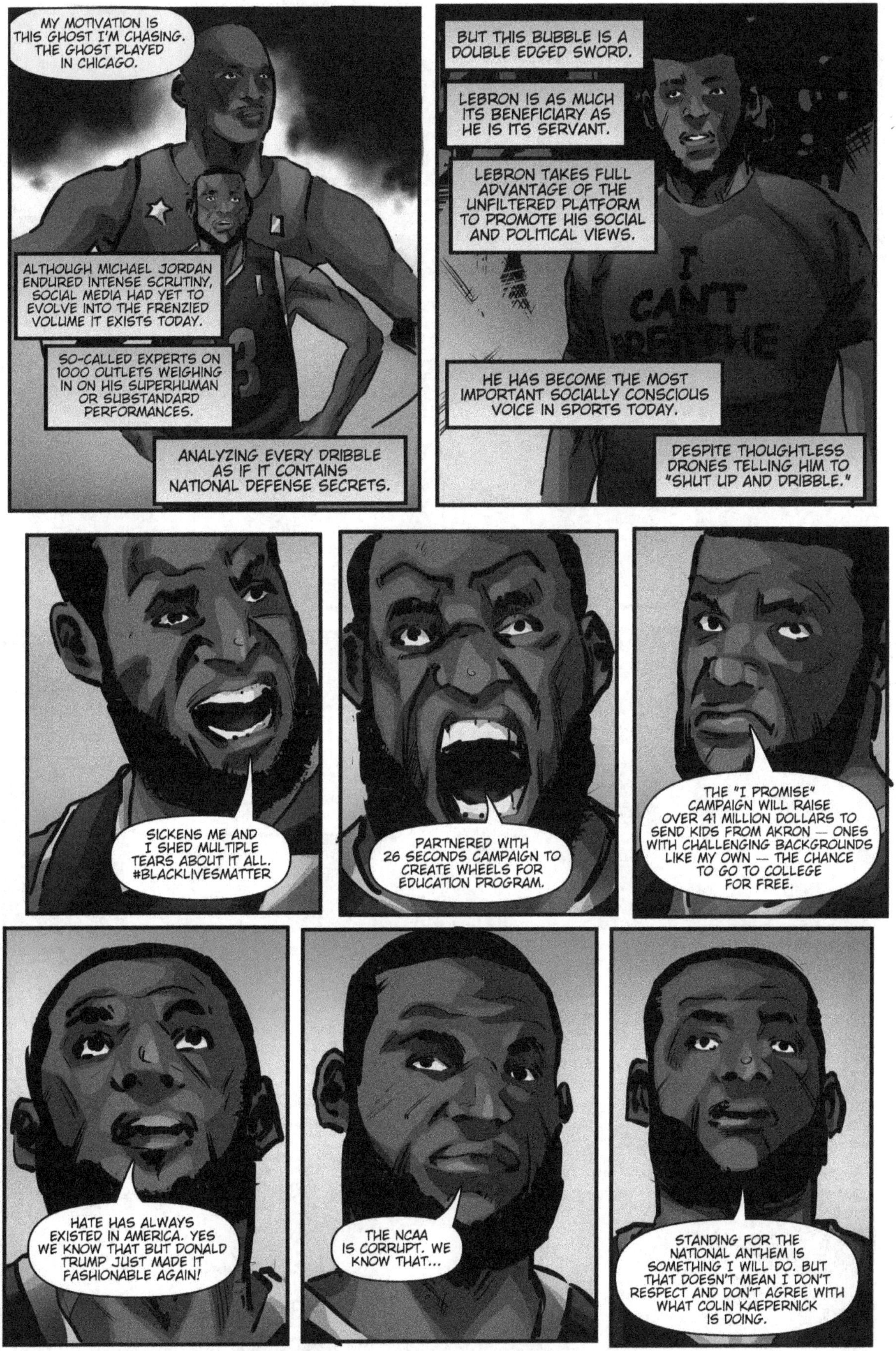
MY MOTIVATION IS THIS GHOST I'M CHASING. THE GHOST PLAYED IN CHICAGO.
ALTHOUGH MICHAEL JORDAN ENDURED INTENSE SCRUTINY, SOCIAL MEDIA HAD YET TO EVOLVE INTO THE FRENZIED VOLUME IT EXISTS TODAY.
SO-CALLED EXPERTS ON 1000 OUTLETS WEIGHING IN ON HIS SUPERHUMAN OR SUBSTANDARD PERFORMANCES.
ANALYZING EVERY DRIBBLE AS IF IT CONTAINS NATIONAL DEFENSE SECRETS.
BUT THIS BUBBLE IS A DOUBLE EDGED SWORD.
LEBRON IS AS MUCH ITS BENEFICIARY AS HE IS ITS SERVANT.
LEBRON TAKES FULL ADVANTAGE OF THE UNFILTERED PLATFORM TO PROMOTE HIS SOCIAL AND POLITICAL VIEWS.
HE HAS BECOME THE MOST IMPORTANT SOCIALLY CONSCIOUS VOICE IN SPORTS TODAY.
DESPITE THOUGHTLESS DRONES TELLING HIM TO "SHUT UP AND DRIBBLE."
SICKENS ME AND I SHED MULTIPLE TEARS ABOUT IT ALL. #BLACKLIVESMATTER
PARTNERED WITH 26 SECONDS CAMPAIGN TO CREATE WHEELS FOR EDUCATION PROGRAM.
THE "I PROMISE" CAMPAIGN WILL RAISE OVER 41 MILLION DOLLARS TO SEND KIDS FROM AKRON — ONES WITH CHALLENGING BACKGROUNDS LIKE MY OWN — THE CHANCE TO GO TO COLLEGE FOR FREE.
HATE HAS ALWAYS EXISTED IN AMERICA. YES WE KNOW THAT BUT DONALD TRUMP JUST MADE IT FASHIONABLE AGAIN!
THE NCAA IS CORRUPT. WE KNOW THAT...
STANDING FOR THE NATIONAL ANTHEM IS SOMETHING I WILL DO. BUT THAT DOESN'T MEAN I DON'T RESPECT AND DON'T AGREE WITH WHAT COLIN KAEPERNICK IS DOING.

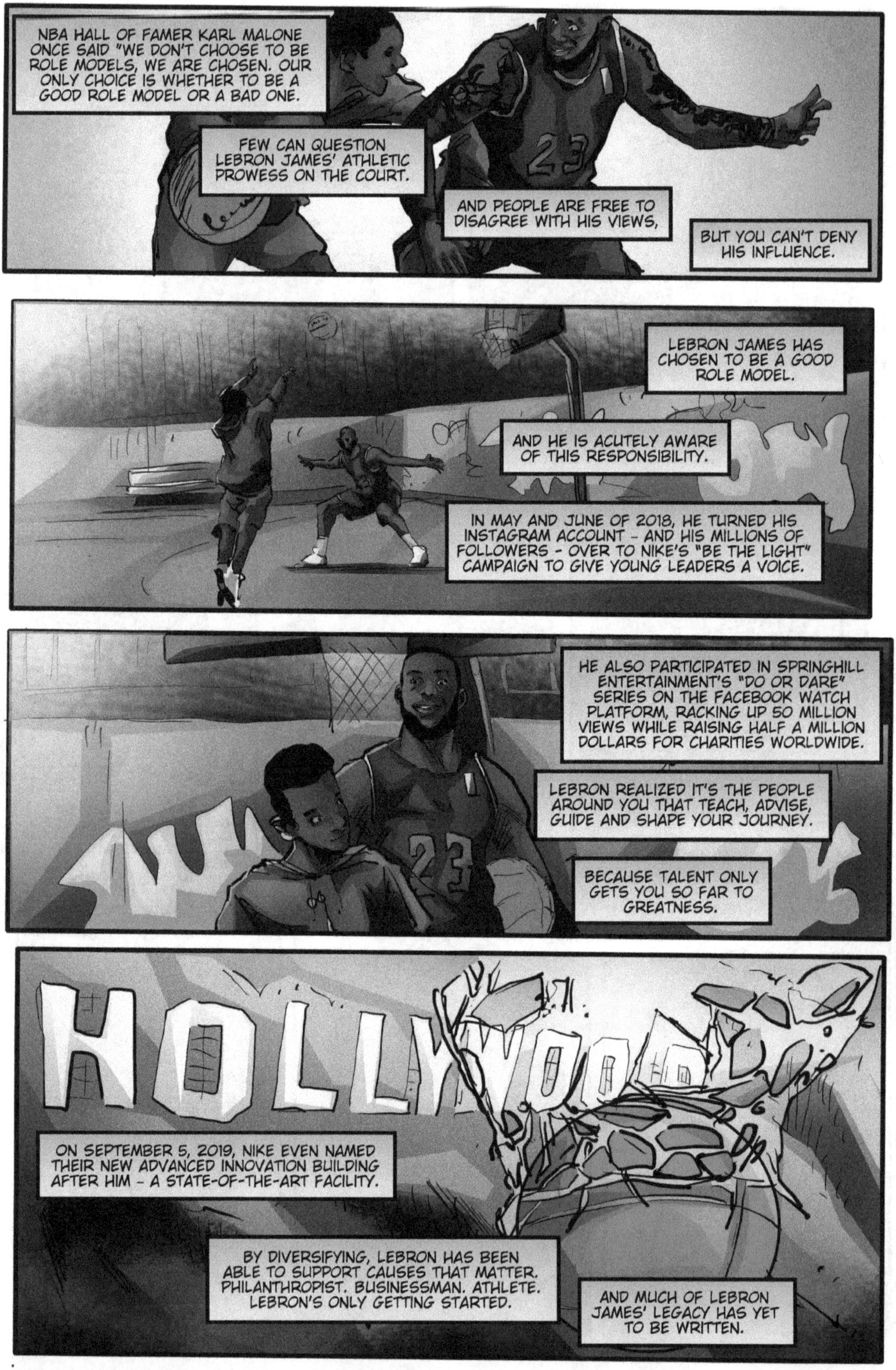
NBA HALL OF FAMER KARL MALONE ONCE SAID "WE DON'T CHOOSE TO BE ROLE MODELS, WE ARE CHOSEN. OUR ONLY CHOICE IS WHETHER TO BE A GOOD ROLE MODEL OR A BAD ONE.
FEW CAN QUESTION LEBRON JAMES' ATHLETIC PROWESS ON THE COURT.
AND PEOPLE ARE FREE TO DISAGREE WITH HIS VIEWS,
BUT YOU CAN'T DENY HIS INFLUENCE.
LEBRON JAMES HAS CHOSEN TO BE A GOOD ROLE MODEL.
AND HE IS ACUTELY AWARE OF THIS RESPONSIBILITY.
IN MAY AND JUNE OF 2018, HE TURNED HIS INSTAGRAM ACCOUNT - AND HIS MILLIONS OF FOLLOWERS - OVER TO NIKE'S "BE THE LIGHT" CAMPAIGN TO GIVE YOUNG LEADERS A VOICE.
HE ALSO PARTICIPATED IN SPRINGHILL ENTERTAINMENT'S "DO OR DARE" SERIES ON THE FACEBOOK WATCH PLATFORM, RACKING UP 50 MILLION VIEWS WHILE RAISING HALF A MILLION DOLLARS FOR CHARITIES WORLDWIDE.
LEBRON REALIZED IT'S THE PEOPLE AROUND YOU THAT TEACH, ADVISE, GUIDE AND SHAPE YOUR JOURNEY.
BECAUSE TALENT ONLY GETS YOU SO FAR TO GREATNESS.
HOLLYWOOD
ON SEPTEMBER 5, 2019, NIKE EVEN NAMED THEIR NEW ADVANCED INNOVATION BUILDING AFTER HIM - A STATE-OF-THE-ART FACILITY.
BY DIVERSIFYING, LEBRON HAS BEEN ABLE TO SUPPORT CAUSES THAT MATTER. PHILANTHROPIST. BUSINESSMAN. ATHLETE. LEBRON'S ONLY GETTING STARTED.
AND MUCH OF LEBRON JAMES' LEGACY HAS YET TO BE WRITTEN.

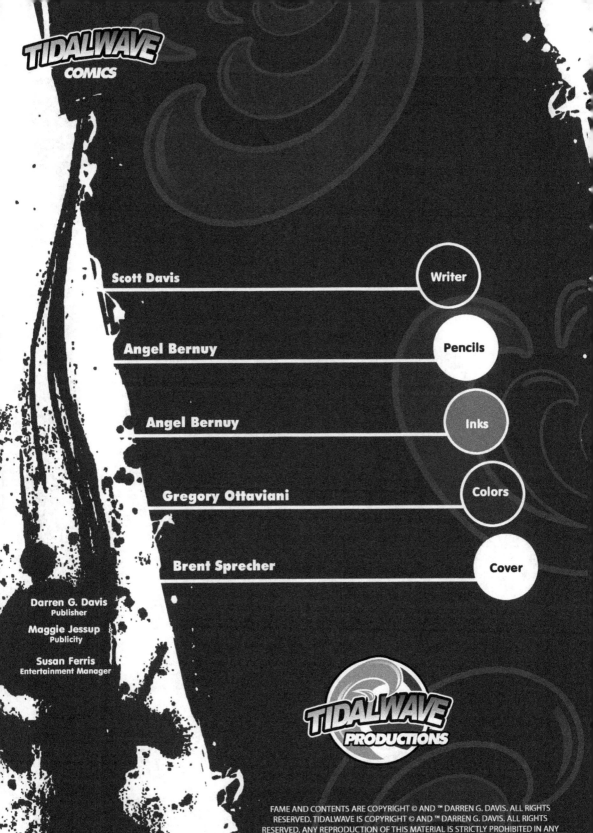

TIDALWAVE COMICS

Scott Davis — Writer

Angel Bernuy — Pencils

Angel Bernuy — Inks

Gregory Ottaviani — Colors

Brent Sprecher — Cover

Darren G. Davis
Publisher

Maggie Jessup
Publicity

Susan Ferris
Entertainment Manager

TIDALWAVE PRODUCTIONS

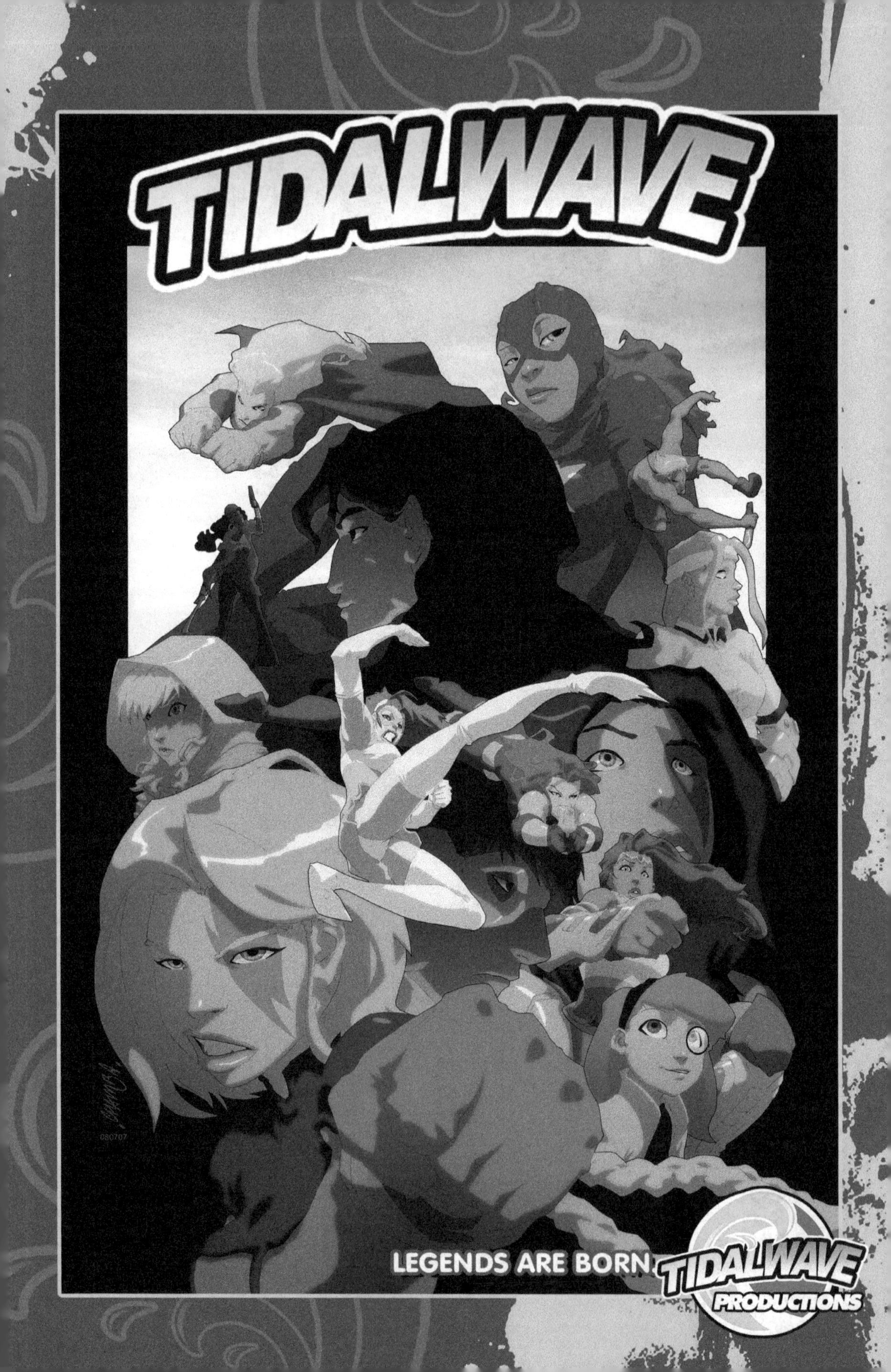
TIDALWAVE
LEGENDS ARE BORN.
TIDALWAVE
PRODUCTIONS

CPSIA information can be obtained
at www.ICGtesting.com
Printed in the USA
LVHW060518281119
638727LV00004B/107/P